PRENTICE-HALL
CONTEMPORARY PERSPECTIVES IN MUSIC EDUCATION SERIES
Charles Leonhard, Editor

Bennett Reimer
A PHILOSOPHY OF MUSIC EDUCATION

Robert Sidnell
BUILDING INSTRUCTIONAL PROGRAMS IN MUSIC EDUCATION

Charles Leonhard
THE ROLE OF METHOD IN MUSIC EDUCATION

Edwin Gordon
THE PSYCHOLOGY OF MUSIC TEACHING

Robert House
ADMINISTRATION IN MUSIC EDUCATION

Richard Colwell
THE EVALUATION OF MUSIC TEACHING AND LEARNING

Clifford K. Madsen and Charles H. Madsen, Jr.
EXPERIMENTAL RESEARCH IN MUSIC

Daniel L. Wilmot
IMPROVING INSTRUCTION IN MUSIC EDUCATION

PRENTICE-HALL INTERNATIONAL, INC., London
PRENTICE-HALL OF AUSTRALIA, PTY. LTD., Sydney
PRENTICE-HALL OF CANADA, LTD., Toronto
PRENTICE-HALL OF INDIA PRIVATE LIMITED, New Delhi
PRENTICE-HALL OF JAPAN, INC., Tokyo

building instructional programs in music education

ROBERT SIDNELL
Department of Music, Michigan State University

PRENTICE-HALL, INC., Englewood Cliffs, New Jersey

Library of Congress Cataloging in Publication Data

SIDNELL, ROBERT.
    Building instructional programs in music education.

    Includes bibliographies.
    1.–School music-Instruction and study-United
States.   I.–Title.
MT3.U5S47   780′.72973   72-8921
ISBN   0-13-087569-4
ISBN: 0-13-087551-1 (pbk.)

Printed in the United States of America

10 9 8 7 6 5 4 3 2 1

foreword

Contemporary Perspectives in Music Education is a new series of professional books for music education. It establishes a pattern for music teacher education based on the areas of knowledge and processes involved in music education rather than on the levels and specializations in music education.

The areas of knowledge include philosophy of music education, psychology of music teaching, and research methods. The processes include program development, instruction, administration, supervision, and evaluation.

The basic premise of the series is that mastery of all of these processes and areas of knowledge is essential for the successful music educator regardless of his area of specialization and the level at which he teaches. The series presents in systematic fashion information and concepts basic to a unified music education profession.

All of the books in the series have been designed and written for use in the undergraduate program of music teacher education. The pattern of the series is both systematic and flexible. It permits music education instructors at the college level to select one or more of the books as texts on the basis of their relevance to a particular course.

The publication of Professor Sidnell's *Building Instructional Pro-*

grams in Music Education represents a landmark in the history of music education in that this book is the first to be concerned exclusively with the process of program development in music education. Its publication is especially fortuitous and timely in view of the current demands for accountability in all areas of education, including music education.

This book is the result of many years of study and research in program development and curriculum construction by Professor Sidnell. Any music educator or group of music educators faced with the task of delineating objectives and selecting experiences for their program will find this book a priceless source of information, insight, and technique.

One of the outstanding characteristics of the book is the manner in which Professor Sidnell has bridged the gap between behavioristic and humanistic points of view toward the music education program. The relationship between these points of view represents one of the major issues in music education now and during the next decade, and this book presents an orientation which will be of great value and assistance to music educators confronting the issue.

Systematic and consistent program development has emerged as the most urgent need of music education at this time in history. This book was conceived and written to fill that need.

Charles Leonhard

preface

This book is designed to set forth a sequence of principles and activities that constitute the curriculum development or program-building process in music education. Essentially, the book deals with instructional planning short of methodology.

The instructional program in music must become increasingly efficient in order to optimize learning in whatever time is awarded music instruction. Efficiency is gained through careful, researched, systematic instructional planning—one of the foremost teacher obligations. Planning is surpassed only by energetic, enthusiastic classroom presentations in the hierarchy of the teacher's art. It is the precise, logical planning that allows the teacher to be sure of outcomes and therefore give meaning and direction to classroom music learning experiences.

Ideally, this book will assist teachers and prospective teachers in defining outcomes, selecting plans of implementation, and creating systems of evaluation. It is reasonable to believe that such care in planning will result in better instructional programs in music for young people. Curricula of quality and balance lead learners to a deeper, more sensitive awareness of music.

Gratitude is due several classes in Music Curriculum Development at Michigan State University for their assistance in bringing this project to life. Similarly, the author's wife, Jo, is an editor of ideas and words, and her aid requires special acknowledgment.

contents

CHAPTER ONE
the music education curriculum   1

CHAPTER TWO
the curriculum development process   20

CHAPTER THREE
determining instructional outcomes   42

CHAPTER FOUR
the content of instruction   61

CHAPTER FIVE
learning experiences and instructional sequence   81

CHAPTER SIX
evaluation: student and program   116

index   146

CHAPTER ONE

the music education curriculum

The music education curriculum is the structure and sequence of music learning experiences in formalized instructional settings. This definition does not dismiss the host of noneducational out-of-school informal musical involvements for learners. On the contrary, extra-school experiences often seem more powerful in shaping musical behaviors than do the efforts of teachers. Unfortunately, music educators have little or no control over nonschool experiences. The immediate problem is the quality, content, and organization of in-school music learning experiences. Curricular experiences in music are supposed to be arranged by the teacher. He manages instruction. He manipulates the learning environment for optimum achievement of predefined objectives. He is a molder and a shaper of musical behavior.

A BACKGROUND

Before assessing the current state of the music education curriculum, it is prudent to review briefly what has gone before. Other men, in other societies, at other times, have contributed to the role of music in education. A brief glance at instructional goals in the past can give perspective and direction to future development and implementation.

The educational process is present in every social organization of man. Among the purposes of education in any culture is the transmission of knowledge to the young. Omnipresent in all educational systems, regardless of how informal, are musical experiences for the young. Music constitutes an important experience for the young because of its cherished place among men as an expression of human feeling that transcends the limitations of direct verbal communication.

In western culture, music has long held a place of importance in education. The Greeks prized music as a means of developing ideal ethical character. Roman civilization found utilitarian values stressing music for the well-rounded citizen participating in government and the military. During the Middle Ages, music was valued as an intensifier of religious experience, particularly for laymen not educated in the letters. During and since the Renaissance, music has been termed the most human of all disciplines, symbolically reflecting the innermost life experiences of men. In the last five centuries, music has been held in high esteem and has been educationally significant for reasons of spiritual value, ethical power, health-giving benefit, disciplinary constraint, therapeutic peace, recreational diversion, and aesthetic power.

Similarly, the music of many nonwestern cultures is retained from generation to generation through formal and informal educational processes. Music for ceremonial rites, festivals, and dances is important for the preservation of identifiable cultural traits. Highly developed musical systems exist in African and Asian cultures in which musical expression for artistic and aesthetic reasons exists beside purely utilitarian ceremonial purposes.

MUSIC EDUCATION IN AMERICA

In American society, music has long been present in the education process. During the colonial century and a half, music instruction was carried on as an extra-school learning activity. Almost all music educators are familiar with the early singing schools and the concerted effort toward increasing the singing and music reading capabilities of the church-going colonists. Soon after Early American society became settled and attention was turned from the frontier, music became an integral part of the school instructional program. This status was achieved by means of an experimental program that was successful in Boston schools in 1837–1838. The teacher was Lowell Mason and the following instructional goals for school music were articulated by a committee of the Boston Board of Education:[1]

1. Intellectually. Music has its place among the seven liberal arts, which scholastic sages regarded as pertaining to humanity. Arithmetic, Geometry, Astronomy, and Music—these formed the quadrivium. Memory, comparison, attention, intellectual faculties—all of them are quickened by a study of its principles. It may be made to some extent a mental discipline.

2. Morally. It is unphilosophical to say that exercises in vocal music may not be so directed and arranged as to produce those habits of feeling of which these sounds are the type. Happiness, contentment, cheerfulness, tranquility—these are the natural effects of music.

3. Physically. It appears self-evident that exercise in vocal music, when not carried to an unreasonable excess, must expand the chest and thereby strengthen the lungs and vital organs. Judging then by this triple standard, intellectually, morally, and physically, vocal music seems to have a natural place in every system of instruction which aspires, as should every system, to develop man's whole nature.

   And in regarding the effect of vocal music, as a branch of popular instruction in our schools, there are some practical considerations which in the opinion of your committee are deserving of particular attention. . . .

   Dynamics, therefore, or that part of vocal music which is concerned with the force and delivery of sounds, has a direct rhetorical connection. In fact the daily sounding of consonant and vowel sounds, deliberately, distinctly, and by themselves, as the committee has heard them sounded in the music lessons given according to the Pestalozzian system of instruction, would, in their opinion, be as good as exercise in the elements of harmonious correct speech as could be imagined.

   An alternation is needed in our schools, which without being idleness shall yet give rest. Vocal music seems exactly fitted to afford that alternation. A recreation, yet not a dissipation of the mind—a respite, yet not a relaxation,—its office would thus be to restore the jaded energies, and send back the scholars with invigorated powers to other more laborious duties.

---

[1] Edward Bailey Birge, *History of Public School Music in the United States*, rev. ed. (Philadelphia: Theodore Presser Company, 1937), pp. 41–43.

These goals typified almost all instructional benefits proclaimed for music curricula at the time. As each individual local school system pioneered a new program of music learning, outcomes and instructional values mirrored those identified by the Boston group.

A brief look at the development of music education in American schools with particular attention on goals and objectives seems prudent. Clearly, current programs of instruction have their roots in the one-hundred-thirty-plus-year history of school music in America.

Birge[2] divides nineteenth-century American music education into three distinct periods of development: The Period of Pioneering (1838–1861); The Beginnings of Method (1861–1885); and The Concentration on Music Reading (1885–1905).

THE PERIOD OF PIONEERING (1838–1861)

In the years immediately before the Civil War, music became an accepted school subject in a limited but influential number of American cities. Nearly always an experimental program preceded full acceptance. In all probability a successful concert provided the final stimulus for hesitating school boards and eager parents/taxpayers. Naturally, early teachers were singing-school leaders and public school instructional programs often replaced and paralleled the colonial Sunday evening singing experience. In fact, there is evidence that in the beginning school music instruction consisted of a transplanted singing-school experience, and in many cases teaching materials were the same.

According to Birge,[3] "The children were taught the elements of music; they became familiar with notes and they learned to read music." This statement probably sums up the goals common to school music at that time. Learning experiences consisted of memorizing verbal facts and learning concepts necessary for music reading achievement. Nonschool music education in the form of Singing Schools and Conventions were still an important facet of American life, particularly in the West. In any event, better singers were the intended outcome of music instruction at the time.

THE BEGINNINGS OF METHOD (1861–1885)

During these years, tremendous growth took place in American musical culture. Instrumental and choral groups made up of native-born

---

2 *Ibid.*, pp. 57–162.

3 *Ibid.*, p. 77.

musicians were formed and became an integral part of society, particularly in the East. Often key players and conductors were recent immigrants, but a somewhat advanced education in music began to be available on this continent. Since society valued music, it was logical to see a parallel growth in the establishment of music instructional programs in the schools.

Early in this period (1873), Luther Whiting Mason compiled the *First Music Reader*.[4] It was an instructional scheme for music that became a prototype for many teaching method books to come. L. W. Mason was not alone in editing a music teacher publication. Nearly all well-known teachers of the time wrote, published, and sold "methods" for music. Primary goals of instructing were the development of the singing voice and teaching music-reading skills using a rote-to-note approach. Also evident during this period were first attempts at instrumental music in the schools. In 1871, a report entitled "Musical Education in Common Schools"[5] contained the following rationale for music in the schools:

Music should enter the common schools education because:

1st   It is an aid to other studies,
2nd   It assists the teacher in maintaining the discipline of the school;
3rd   It cultivates the aesthetic nature of the child,
4th   It is valuable as a means of mental discipline,
5th   It lays a favorable foundation for the more advanced culture of later life,
6th   It is a positive economy,
7th   It is of the highest value as a sanitary measure,
8th   It prepares for participation in the church service.

And again, through the medium of the music lesson the moral nature of the child may be properly cultivated.

Certainly not all of the above goals enjoyed implementation through curricular experiences in music. More than likely, all music instructional programs were directed to the singing and music reading goals identified by Luther W. Mason.

CONCENTRATION UPON MUSIC READING (1885–1905)

This period saw curricular experiences for children which led to music reading competence. Reading was the one great music education

---

4 Luther Whiting Mason, *First Music Reader* (Boston: Ginn and Co., 1873).

5 Eben F. Tourjee, "Musical Education in Common Schools," *Report of the Commissioner of Education, 1871* (Washington, D.C.: U.S. Bureau of Education, 1871), p. 536.

objective of the period. Rote singing, popular during the previous period, became taboo and singing for enjoyment was supposedly nonexistent. The curriculum was made up of experiences in pitch and rhythm drills aimed at developing music reading competence. Curricular activities reported for grades 3, 4, and 5 of the Minneapolis Schools in 1896 are shown in Table 1.1.[6]

Numerous methods and publications of drills appeared during this period. School teachers were indoctrinated to the dogma of various supervisors through summer workshops, institutes, and normal courses.

At the turn of the century, goals for music education were articulated by Herbart Griggs in a paper delivered to the music committee of the National Educational Association. He stated, "Music when properly taught should accomplish the following results:

1. Mentally, a quickening of the perceptive faculties through exercise in rapid discovery, recognition, and concentration.
2. Physically, through exercise in breathing tone production, correct posture of the body, and of the saturation of the body and mind with sonorous fluid.
3. Disciplinary, through doing the same thing, in the same way, at the same time, and the effect of sustained tone and harmony on the mind thus dissipating the spirit of contradiction.
4. Morally, by creating a love for the good and beautiful in music. . . ."[7]

The similarity between the Griggs statement and those goals originally articulated by the Boston School board in 1838 is noteworthy.

By 1917, four generalized instructional outcomes were set down by Earhart and McConathy in a report for the Commissioner of Education.[8] They listed aesthetic, socializing, avocational, and vocational benefits as chief aims of music education. In the same report the authors recommended the following classes in music for specific amounts of credit in the High School:[9]

Chorus	Music Appreciation
Orchestra	Theory of Music (Harmony and Counterpoint)
Glee Club	Applied Music

---

6 O. E. McFadon, "Report of the Music Department," *Addresses and Proceedings of the National Education Association, Buffalo, New York, 1896* (Chicago: University of Chicago Press, 1897), p. 753.

7 Herbart Griggs, "Report of the Music Department, *"Addresses and Proceedings of the National Education Association, Los Angeles, 1899* (Chicago: University of Chicago Press, 1899), pp. 977–78.

8 Will Earhart and Osbourne McConathy, *Music in the Secondary Schools, Bulletin #49* (Washington, D.C.: U.S. Bureau of Education, 1917), pp. 12–14.

9 *Ibid.,* p. 33.

Table 1.1 Music Curricular Activities in the Minneapolis Schools (1896).

	Third Grade	Fourth Grade	Fifth Grade
1. Teacher point, class name line or space (no.). Repeat rapidly abcdefg, defgabc, cdefgab, etc. Repeat rapidly c,g,b,d,f and f,a,c,e. Teacher point line or space, class name tone represented. Teacher name tone, class name line or space which represents it (1st line, 2d space, etc.)	Commenced and Completed.		
2. Write scales without signature. Write scales with signature.	Commenced.	Continued.	Continued.
3. Sing given scale by letter daily.	Continued. Scale on Board without Signature.	Continued. Scale on Board without Signature.	Continued. Scale on Board with Signature.
4. Chromatic tones and scales.		Commenced. Sharps.	Continued.
5. Teacher dictate tones by letter, class sing syllables.		Commenced.	Continued, including Chromatic Sharps.
6. Modulation.		Commenced.	Continued. Oblique.
7. The terms "diatonic" and "chromatic."			Completed.
8. How to write sharps upon the staff.		Commenced.	Completed.
9. How to write flats upon the staff.		Commenced.	Commenced.
10. Teacher call tones by number, class sing by syllable. Name tones (letter-name) when called upon.			

Fifteen years later a report in a similar office of Education Bulletin indicated the following results of a nationwide survey on stated objectives of Music Education:[10]

Objective	Frequency of Mention
Social	56
Singing	51
Discipline	44
Vocational	38
Aesthetic	36
Leisure	31
Physical	25
Emotional	24
Ethical	18
Instrumental	9
Creative	5
Interest	4

More specific instructional objectives were also recorded in the same document. From these one can infer what learning experiences may have been, at least in the schools that responded to the survey. Ann Pierce listed the following in the 1933 Report:

Activity	Frequency of Mention
Sight Singing	68
Familiarity with Composers and Music	65
Part Singing	63
Improved Vocal Habits	49
Notation	44
Form Study	35
Enlarged Repertoire	29
Study of Instruments	27
Choral Singing	24
Correlation	10
Kinds of Songs	8

By 1946, the MENC Committee on Elementary School Music Curricula articulated the following as most important outcomes for music instruction:[11]

---

[10] Ann E. Pierce and Robert S. Hilpert, *Instruction in Music and Art, Bulletin #17* (Washington, D.C., Office of Education, 1932), p. 7.

[11] Committee on Elementary School Music Curricula, "Report," *Music Educators Journal* (March, 1946), p. 32.

a. To help the child secure his correct singing voice; develop rhythmic responses to music through free bodily movement; develop an interest in instrumental music; develop genuine love for and appreciation of good music.

b. To increase desire to participate in music activities.

c. To lead children to self-expression through music.

d. To develop musical skills and understandings.

e. To find talent and provide for its development.

Suggested experiences to implement these goals included:

Singing Experiences

1. Song repertoire of musically interesting and worthwhile rote materials that (a) suits the child's age and experience; (b) presents gradual sequence from simple, short songs to those more difficult melodically and rhythmically; (c) integrates with school and home experiences; (d) is cumulative and will function in the experience of living.

2. Diagnosis and cure by individual attention of children who present vocal problems.

3. Music reading-readiness program that meets the needs of varying groups and bridges the rote-note process successfully.

4. Introduction of the score as means to the end of a continuing and expanding song repertoire that will make a nation of musical literates.

5. Acquaintance with great composers and artists through the music sung.

6. Participation in special choir or glee club by selected students.

Listening Experiences

1. Listening to songs to learn words and melody.

2. Listening to instrumental music in order to experience rhythmic expression.

3. Listening to "live" or recorded music for (a) joy it affords; (b) acquaintance with musical literature; (c) development of discrimination and critical judgment; (d) understanding of the form of music; (e) understanding of great musical personalities of present and past.

Rhythmic Experiences

1. Bodily responses to music of simple rhythms such as walking, running, skipping, jumping, etc.

2. Imitative response, creating rhythms and dramatizations in response to music of varying moods.

3. Directed rhythmic responses in singing games and folk dances.

4. Simple patterns in rhythmic responses into note and rest values in music notation.

Playing Experiences

1. Opportunity for playing in the rhythm orchestra.
2. Play toy flutes or other pre-orchestral instruments.
3. Pupils may take class piano or instrumental lessons.
4. In upper elementary grades pupils begin to play in school orchestras.

Creative Experiences

1. Setting words to music, either familiar or original verses.
2. Composing tunes for special occasions, dramatizations, etc.
3. Devising new forms in dancing.

Within the last several decades, music educators have reached never before attained heights of performance competence with school musicians. Partly because of extensive group instruction techniques, bands, orchestras, and choruses, in addition to small ensembles of all kinds, have provided challenging and creative experiences for the talented child. There is little doubt that motivated and gifted students have been found and given ample opportunities for music learning.

Typical music education programs now embrace some of the following philosophical positions either singly or in an interconnected manner from the very conservative music reading-centered curriculum of 1900:

1. *Appreciation.* Teach the love of music through listening.
2. *Activities.* Sing, play, move, create, and listen where the activity itself becomes the objective.
3. *Integrated/Correlated.* Find ways to use music to enhance other subject areas.
4. *Concept Centered.* Within the structure of musical knowledge lie certain truths that generate the important objectives of musical learning.
5. *Aesthetic/Humanistic.* A profound human experience that can be heightened and magnified through increased perceptual awareness.
6. *Performance Training.* Teach those capable of performing with the highest accuracy.
7. *Social.* Music as an expression of man in society (a multiplicity of miniature societies in parent culture).
8. *Ethnic.* Study of music of many cultures as a basis for understanding man's attempt to symbolize human experience in tone.

Classes which constitute the music education curriculum are collections of experiences, in many cases unrelated, supposed to serve predetermined goals. In a comprehensive school system curriculum might be evident by the following class labels:

Elementary: General Music, Piano Class, Keyboard Experience Classes, Wind Instrument Instruction, String Instruction.

Middle or Junior High School: General Music, Choir, Band, Orchestra, Glee Club, Humanities, Beginning Instrumental Class.

High School: General Music, Humanities, Music Appreciation, Music Theory, Allied Arts, Band, Orchestra, Jazz Band, Chamber Music, Chorus, A cappela Choir and Glee Clubs.

Perhaps the most lucid recent statement of goals for music education that would be implemented by instruction in the above classes is contained in a publication of the Music Educators National Conference. Ernst identified three broad categories of goals and listed several model outcomes under each.[12]

Skills

1. He will have skill in listening to music.
2. He will be able to sing.
3. He will be able to express himself on a musical instrument.
4. He will be able to interpret musical notation.

Understandings

5. He will understand the importance of design in music.
6. He will relate music to man's historical development.
7. He will understand the relationship existing between music and other areas of human endeavor.
8. He will understand the place of music in contemporary society.

Attitudes

9. He will value music as a means of self-expression.
10. He will desire to continue his musical experiences.
11. He will discriminate with respect to music.

Ernst continues and indicates content should include the following topics: Elements of Music, Form and Design, Interpretive Aspects, Acoustics, Musical Score, Historical Considerations, Music and Man, Music as a Form of Expression, Types of Music Performance, Music in Humanities, Music Today.

In summary, school music in America has come a long way since its inception in 1838. The record is not perfect, but progress has been steady and noteworthy. One should recall that it is a great first-time experiment for a society to support music instruction to the extent that it has been in America. Recent statistics indicate four million children and adolescents are now engaged in music-making in our schools. From two

---

12 Karl Ernst and Charles Gary, *Music in General Education* (Washington, D.C.: *Music Educators National Conference,* 1965), pp. 4–8.

experimental schools in Boston there are now approximately 93% of all schools in America having something called an organized instructional program in music.

ASSESSING MUSIC EDUCATION

Notable music education programs are usually identified by outstanding performance groups that provide unprecedented opportunities for skill development of talented students. School bands, choirs, and orchestras are points of great pride in many communities. There is no reason to minimize the great contribution these performing groups make to learners, schools, and communities. In fact, one of the most distinctive dimensions of American public education can easily be the performing music ensemble aspect of the curriculum. In the main, the growth and success of these groups are directly related to the almost superhuman dedication and service of music educators. Countless hours of effort and unwavering perseverance provide the base upon which successful performing groups rest. Approximately 15% of all students in high schools in America are privileged to participate in music performing groups. Taxpayers usually support levies that produce funds for the continuance of well-established music performing groups. The remaining 85% of high school students do not have equal opportunities to participate in substantial music experiences. This group provides the target population for general instructional programs in music. The music attitudes of this group are in a large measure responsible for the survival and cultivation of musical culture in this society. What the nonperformers think about music and its value in life has to be of prime concern for every music educator. The current educational program in music available to the nonperformer is not all that it should be. There is room for improvement to equalize levels of excellence with performing groups.

WHAT NEEDS TO BE CHANGED

In general, instructional programs in music suffer from three basic shortcomings:

1. vagueness of purpose,
2. misplaced emphasis,
3. lack of sequence.

Vagueness of purpose. It is common to find a series of capricious music activities masquerading as a music curriculum. Learners very often *enjoy* this kind of music participation but little if any substantial learning takes place. Some music educators are satisfied with pupil enjoyment as a *raison d'etre*—they teach for the moment. Few, if any, human beings need educational experiences to find enjoyment in some kind of music. There is really nothing wrong with enjoyment, but to identify such a nebulous, superficial goal as foremost for music education is inappropriate. There are certainly occasions when being involved with music eventuates in a clear feeling of enjoyment. However, there is much more derivable benefit when participation becomes more sophisticated. For example, students probably enjoy music performance classes for a multitude of nonmusical reasons. This is simply because learners do not have the musical sophistication to react musically to the stimuli present. Social goals are more easily identified and attained by pupils. Performing classes provide a novel means for peer group togetherness. Vagueness of purpose can also become manifest when music education pretends to serve such nonmusical goals as:

1. Music education promotes self-discipline.
2. Music education is conducive to sound mental health.
3. Music education fosters development of social responsibility.

The above goals are not all wrong but certainly they cannot be considered germane to the process of music education. Music has something unique to offer—life enrichment through aesthetic sensitivity. Goals not associated with the essence of the music experience cannot be appropriately identified as primary for music education. A well-conceived program of music instruction will by its nature promote music enjoyment but the greatest joy for students should accrue from the music learning process itself rather than be dependent on simple group involvement.

Misplaced emphasis. Nearly all music classes in schools today do not provide substantial learning experiences for pupils. Often students merely undergo and endure. This is particularly manifest in performance classes. The band, orchestra, and choir should be learning experiences for students. However, the teacher/conductor is probably most involved and brings a highly refined set of behaviors to the experience. His auditory perception is much keener. He has appropriate ways to organize sounds into meaningful patterns. He can identify repetitions in melody and gain clarity to the overall form of a composition. He knows something about the style of the period the music may represent. In short, he possesses sophisticated musical behaviors that make his experience meaningful. But what of the students? By and large, they do not possess this degree of musical understanding. Are these skills and knowledge so secret and precious that only those with college majors in music can have access? The purpose of the class is to contribute a vocabulary of musical skills, knowledge, perception, and attitudes to learners.

The situation in so-called nonperformance classes is much worse. Here there is not even a chance for accidental learning. In a performance class some gains in musical literacy can accidentally accrue, but in the usual general music class there is little chance for substantial gains. Yet the most singular outcome of the general class is to develop usable aural music literacy in the nonperformer. The very essence of this course is to foster the growth of listening skills and clear understanding of musical structure.

A program of music education must provide for the continuing development of music skills and knowledge that will promote a growing urbanity of music behavior. Classes do not constitute curriculum. It is the experience of doing, involvement, and problem solving with music that form the curriculum. Experiences, then, are the essence. Emphasis must be on the quality of the experience and its sequential arrangement. Performance is not wrong, not remotely wrong. True realization of music comes from performance; there is no suitable vicarious substitute. Misdirected, careless performance is inappropriate. Conductor/teachers can provide for optimum musical development during the performance experience if they take a little care in planning total and varied musical experiences for students.

Lack of sequence. At present there is little evidence of measurable differences in musical growth from year to yar. Stages of musical growth are equally ill-defined. A fifth-grader often does not exhibit musical behaviors substantially different from a fourth-grader. Should he? There is little experimental evidence that identifies sequential musical growth in any school music program. Music education is not blessed with an abundance of researchers inclined toward longitudinal growth studies. No research findings identify the long-term roles of maturation and training in musical growth and development. The few existent facts come from studies of children in atypical learning situations (lab schools, clinical situations). One study in public high schools indicated only very small differences in musical achievement between students enrolled in music performance groups and those not so enrolled (Folstrom, 1966).[13] Another notable exception is Gordon's Five-Year Study of Musical Growth now nearing completion.[14] Clearly, there are measurement problems re-

---

[13] Roger J. Folstrom, "A Comparative Study of the Musical Achievement of Students in Three Illinois High Schools" (unpublished Doctoral dissertation, Northwestern University, 1967).

[14] Edwin Gordon, "The Third Year of a Five Year Longitudinal Study of Musical Growth (unpublished paper, The University of Iowa, Iowa City).

lated to the instruments available for assessment. Recent developments in test construction (Colwell, 1969; Gordon, 1967) promise greater precision than heretofore possible in assessing both achievement and potential of school-aged young people.

Aside from research studies, there is a similar paucity of courses of study and curriculum guides that *precisely* define outcomes and sequence of objectives. A survey by Arberg[15] notes the existence of 321 courses of study. Those that do exist usually lack clear statement of goals and offer little evidence of sequential learning. Although available materials probably have little value beyond local origin, the fact that some music staffs have achieved instructional design of one sort or another is encouraging. State level plans also lack clear sequence and can only offer general guidelines to local systems. Notable exceptions include Kentucky, New Jersey, Florida, Georgia, and Michigan.

The Kentucky Music Education Association has an extensive list of terminal objectives for music education. The Association has attempted to define musical behaviors that may be expected to accrue from the common twelve-year school instructional program. The Committee states that the list includes

> . . . the musical behaviors that may be expected to result from the common twelve years of elementary and secondary instruction. Students who elect specialized instruction, such as band, orchestra, chorus, music theory, or music literature, may be expected to exhibit other behaviors in addition to these. Ultimately, lists of objectives for each grade level and for each specialized field should be established on the basis of these terminal objectives . . . .
>
> That the percentages and the objectives themselves will be subjected to continuous examination and revision. The criteria may be established by the individual percentages. In this manner an appropriate list of objectives consistent with the local philosophy curriculum and needs can be arrived at by every school district regardless of its economic, social or demographic status.

Objectives are classified as follows:

I. Cognitive
  A. Terminology
  B. Symbols
  C. Media

---

15 Harold W. Arberg and Sarah P. Wood, Music Curriculum Guides (Washington, D.C.: U.S. Department of Health, Education and Welfare, 1964), 1964.

        D. Structure
        E. Creating
        F. Cultural background

II. Psychomotor
        A. Singing
        B. Playing

III. Affective
        A. Listening
        B. Participation
        C. Discrimination
        D. Commitment

A typical objective reads:

Cognitive-Structure

After three hearings of a two-part polyphonic excerpt, be able to determine whether a given melodic or rhythmic motive, heard separately, occurred in the excerpt, did not occur, or occurred in modified form.[16]

Tentative goals for a twelve-year music curriculum in Michigan includes:

1. Develop musical skills to enrich his life.
2. Acquire knowledge and understanding of music from all historical periods, styles, forms and cultures and various functions of music in contemporary, pluralistic society.
3. Make rational choices in musical situations, e.g., judge quality of musical performance.
4. Respond with feeling to the expressive elements and line of the music.[17]

Three categories are thus indicated: skill, knowledge, and aesthetic sensitivity. One elementary school program objective might be:

Given an aural musical example, the student shall describe the music in terms of the elements (melody, harmony, tonality, rhythm, tempo, dynamics, timbre), texture, form, function and/or style.

---

16 Kentucky Music Education Committee on Music Education in Kentucky, "Objectives of Music Education" (unpublished document, 1969), pp. 2–6.

17 Michigan Music Education Association, "Tentative Goals of Music Education in Michigan" (unpublished document, 1971).

More states are developing statements of minimum achievement at the completion of school which outline precise, measurable accomplishment. Music education must make a difference in people if it is to survive. Some differences will readily be measurable; others will be evidenced in less overt behavior patterns.

WHAT CAN BE DONE

Music educators are often inclined to identify school administrators as causes for unsatisfactory teaching conditions. Truly, foremost among the administrator's responsibilities is facilitating instruction. Many times, in the case of music, an administrator can ask honestly, "What instruction?" On the other hand, teacher complaints regarding scheduling, poor budget, unsuitable facilities, and insufficient equipment are legitimate. The relationship between the two extremes may be very strong. A program that lacks accountability will not find strong support at the administrative level. If those responsible for school policy see only the public relations value of music, one can expect little aid in supporting a true instructional program. However, if the music staff can function cooperatively to forge a solid, well-organized program with observable benefits to all students, the administrators must pay heed. The development of such a program is a significant part of the teacher's responsibility. The case for music must be proven. Music education needs regeneration, redirection, innovation, and continued program involvement with solid evaluation as a base. The music staff is responsible for the music curriculum. A cooperative, alive group of music educators must produce a sequentially organized instructional program with clearly defined outcomes. No one at the administrative level will do it.

At this point it must be clear that there is the need for curriculum reform and development. This book is not a treatise on the ills of music education. Major problems have been identified to support the urgency for full-scale curriculum development. There is, at present, a music curriculum. Students do become involved with music. All is not bad or in need of complete overhaul. If teaching staffs can see the need for renovation and change, there is a place to begin. Curriculum building should be a never-ending process of defining goals, implementing procedures, and evaluating process and product. We live in an ever-changing society. Instructional programs in schools can never remain static and survive. As one writer points out,

> values, ideas, knowledge, and ways of life change rapidly, so young people must be prepared to cope with these changes.

The changes in society have implications for the public school curriculum, which must change and keep pace with society and its demands.[18]

SUMMARY

The music education program was defined as the structure and sequence of music learning experiences in formalized instructional settings. A brief review of the place of music in education was noted with particular emphasis on goals that have identified instructional intent in American Music Education. Recent activity in processes for developing more precise statements of instructional outcomes has generated a number of statements more complete in detail relative to music education curriculum. Some of the problems of current music education programs were identified and listed as vagueness of purpose, misplaced emphasis, and lack of sequence. It is through the curriculum development process that stronger, more accountable programs of instruction can be instituted.

ACTIVITIES FOR DISCUSSION AND STUDY

1. Gather lists of goals for music education from local school systems or from the general public.
2. Identify differences between current and nineteenth-century goals in music education.
3. Compile a bibliography of research that documents musical growth in any way.
4. Consult historical dissertations in music education that deal with "pioneers" in the field. Assemble a glossary of their goals for music education.
5. Assess the music curriculum from the school system in which you received your training. Indicate points of weakness and strength.
6. Visit a school system in order to determine whether or not there are any noteworthy innovations in its music curriculum.
7. Develop, in writing, your own definition of music curriculum.

---

[18] John R. Verduin, Jr., *Cooperative Curriculum Improvement* (Englewood Cliffs, N.J.: Prentice-Hall, Inc., 1967), p. 2.

SUPPLEMENTARY READINGS

Arberg, Harold, and Sarah P. Wood, *Music Curriculum Guides*, Bulletin No. 14. Washington, D.C.: U.S. Department of Health, Education, and Welfare, 1964.

Birge, Edward Bailey, *History of Public School Music in the United States* (3rd. ed.). Washington, D.C.: Music Educators National Conference, 1966.

Britton, Allen, "Music in Early American Education," *Basic Concepts in Music Education*. Chicago: The University of Chicago Press, 1958, pp. 195–214.

Ernst, Karl, and Charles Gary, *Music in General Education*. Washington, D.C.: Music Educators National Conference, 1966.

Kowall, Bonnie C., *Perspectives in Music Education Sourcebook III*. Washington, D.C.: Music Educators National Conference, 1966.

Leonhard, Charles, and Robert House, *Foundations and Principles of Music Education* (rev. ed.). New York: McGraw-Hill Book Company, 1972.

CHAPTER TWO

the curriculum development process

In recent years there has been a massive curriculum reform movement in American schools. New instructional programs have been developed in math, physics, biology, chemistry, geography, and foreign languages. Teachers of all levels have joined in the formulation of new materials. Elementary and secondary students have participated in data gathering programs for countless studies in the trial of new learning strategies. The sciences were first to experience extensive reshaping. More recently, there is emphasis on the social sciences, humanities, and arts. This shift in emphasis is caused by the realization that the sciences have had high priority in funding from such sources as the National Science Foundation and the U.S. Office of Education. More than one writer has commented on this imbalance and has suggested that "projects in the social sciences and humanities be given priorities."[1]

Aside from changes in specific subject areas, the process of curriculum development itself has experienced unique changes in emphasis. In the 1960's an almost violent swing to behaviorism and application of

---

[1] John Goodlad, *School Curriculum Reform in the United States* (New York: The Fund for the Advancement of Education, 1964), p. 77.

systems design resulted in what some writers identified as behavioral engineering. This movement culminated in an extreme form of accountability labeled contracting. This process, conducted by both educational and noneducational agencies, provided a supposedly sure-fire way to reach prearranged objectives. The whole behavioral movement probably stemmed from the work of Tyler[2] and Herrick[3] in the early 1950's. More recent contributions by Mager,[4] Yelon,[5] Popham,[6] Taba,[7] Banathy,[8] and Woodruff[9] have brought greater levels of precision in the process of curriculum development.

WHAT ABOUT MUSIC EDUCATION?

Where does music education stand? One writer suggests "that a new look at the entire area of secondary general music is indeed in order —at least as much as has seemed necessary for other subjects and perhaps even more so."[10] One cannot quarrel with this position, but secondary general music is only one vehicle of musical growth. Teachers of music are going to have to look at the total instructional program. Music educators must be the architects of music learning. A first responsibility is the development of a means by which young people can grow in music skills, knowledge, and awareness. To do this the music educator is allocated varying amounts of instructional time depending on the nature of the class. These instructional periods are precious chunks of time. A teacher must be judicious in how that time is used. It is not only advantageous but necessary to know where learners have been, where they are going, and where they are to end. The teacher must be aware of his part in the music learning continuum. There should be a growth curve that repre-

---

[2] Ralph Tyler, *Basic Principles of Curriculum and Instruction* (Chicago: The University of Chicago Press, 1950).

[3] Virgil Herrick, *Strategies of Curriculum Development,* compiled by D. W. Andersen, J. B. MacDonald, and F. B. May (Columbus, Ohio: C. E. Merrill Books, 1965).

[4] Robert F. Mager. *Preparing Instructional Objectives* (Palo Alto: Fearon Publishers, 1962).

[5] Stephen Yelon and Roger O. Scott, *A Strategy for Writing Objectives* (Dubuque: Kendall/Hunt, 1970).

[6] W. J. Popham and E. I. Baker, *Establishing Instructional Goals* (Englewood Cliffs, N.J.: Prentice-Hall, Inc., 1970).

[7] Hilda Taba, *Curriculum Development Theory and Practice* (New York: Harcourt, Brace & World, Inc.) 1962.

[8] Bela Banathy, *Instructional Systems* (Palo Alto: Fearon Publishers, 1968).

[9] Asahel Woodruff, "Concept Teaching in Music," *Perspectives in Music Education* (Washington, D.C.: Music Educators National Conference, 1966).

[10] Bennett Reimer, "The Curriculum Reform Movement and the Problem of Secondary General Music," *Music Educators Journal* (January, 1966), p. 41.

sents evolving musical sophistication. To be conscious of, with reasonable approximation, where learners are in music development can help to insure the wise use of instructional time. The sequencing of all music learning experiences into a unified, logical program of instruction is a responsibility of the first order. Instructional organization constitutes a significant part of the teacher's art. Moreover, this process is a total music staff obligation. For the most part the task is undone. If music education is going to make a difference, curriculum development and instructional reorganization are mandatory. Learners must have careful direction in a sequence of music experiences that provides a base for lasting involvement with music. Music education should make a difference in the lives of an individual both as student and graduate. The quality of an individual's existence should be a prime target of the music education process. In-school experiences are important to shape lifelong attitudes. There is joy to be had from participation in music-making peers—second-graders singing a round or high-school bandsmen performing a Holst Suite. However, since music is a time art, such pleasure only serves the moment. What of the time after formal schooling is completed? Can the learner function independently in a musical experience?

What is it to be musically educated? A musically educated person can be defined as one who has the ability to perceive, assimilate, and sort musical stimuli intelligently and to participate independently in a musical experience. This individual usually finds ways to use music in his life functionally, either as an active participant or as an intellectually active listener. He demonstrates approach behavior to music, thus seeking music involvement for himself and for those close to him.

The need for dynamic programs in music curriculum development is clear. Evidence of awareness among music educators does exist. Presessions at regional and national conventions dedicated to certain steps in the curriculum development process have been initiated. If, however, music education is to survive, there is need to examine the process of curriculum development in detail. There are many decisions to be made. What course of action should be followed? What should be taught? How can objectives be clearly defined? Sequence of learning should be identified. Strategies need definition and the quality of learning experiences demands careful scrutiny. A total review and possible redirection of the music curricula is in order. A clear understanding of the curriculum development process is indeed indispensable.

CURRICULUM DEVELOPMENT

The field of curriculum development is a relative latecomer as an educational specialty. Before 1920 there is practically no mention of the curriculum specialist or the program development process. Courses of study, based on existent textbooks, formed the curriculum. All goals and objectives were related to subject matter areas which provided the base for all education in America. Educational process was this way because the schools are the instrument of a society for its perpetuation and future development. What goes on in the school is subject to pressure from society. According to one curriculum specialist, school instruction programs have been subject to pressure from four social motives:[11]

1. *The Religious (1635–1770)*. Aim was to build a society based on religious principles and to inculcate these tenets in the young through schools.
2. *The Political (1770–1860)*. Aim was to develop a literate population which could participate in a democratic form of government.
3. *The Utilitarian (1860–1920)*. With the rise of pragmatism, public education turned toward vocational and technical training high schools with greater expanded subject offerings.
4. *Mass Education (1920–present)*. Supposed equalized educational opportunity for all children.

These motives have produced discernible differences in school curricula. Most evident are the changes in subjects taught at both the elementary and secondary levels. As noted, prior to 1920 there is little written regarding the curriculum development process. During the 1920's and 1930's superintendents in large systems assumed the authority for curriculum planning. They selected committees, usually headed by an assistant superintendent or supervisor, to develop "curricula." Curricula during those years was believed to be and often was defined as the content of courses of study by subject matter. Beginning in the late 1930's, a gradual shift in ideas relative to the meaning of curriculum improvement became evident. It was no longer autocratic, administration-dominated. Textbooks and teaching materials were no longer chosen as the basis of the curriculum. Following the shift from an administrator-dominated process, curriculum development began to embrace the following basic points of view:

1. Curriculum development is an ongoing activity.
2. Teachers assume important roles in curriculum development either through planning, writing, organizing, or evaluating.
3. Curriculum development involves a large span of activity: assess, write, implement, experiment, evaluate.

---

[11] J. Minor Gwynn, *Curriculum Principles and Social Trends*, 3rd ed. (New York: The Macmillan Company, 1960), pp. 1–35.

4. Laymen are asked to participate in a general way but cannot be expected to solve professional problems.[12]

Curriculum development has been defined as a process which

"needs to draw upon the analyses of society and culture, studies of the learner and the learning process and analysis of the nature of knowledge in order to determine the purposes of the school and the nature of its curriculum."[13]

Almost all writers agree in spirit with the above definition. What a school curriculum contains is in part dependent on what society demands, what learners can do, and what material is available for study and experiences. These same points were delineated by Tyler[14] in the form of questions. In turn, these questions became the basic outline of the curriculum development process. Tyler asked:

1. What educational purposes should the school seek to attain?
2. What educational experiences can be provided that are likely to attain these purposes?
3. How can these educational experiences be effectively organized?
4. How can we determine whether these purposes are being attained?

In response to Tyler's first question, there is no paucity of goal statements for American schools. Doll iterated the following as chief goals:[15]

1. To develop learners intellectually.
2. To develop learners as functioning citizens.
3. To develop learners as individuals in our society.
4. To develop learners as actual or potential workers.

Compare the above 1970 goals with those formulated in 1918[16] and 1938.[17]

---

12 Ronald C. Doll, *Decision Making and Process*, 2nd ed. (Boston: Allyn and Bacon, Inc., 1970), p. 22.

13 Taba, *op. cit.*, p. 10.

14 Tyler, *op. cit.*, pp. 1–2.

15 Doll, *op. cit.*, pp. 16–17.

16 Commission for the Reorganization of Secondary Education, *The Cardinal Principles of Secondary Education* (Washington, D.C.: U.S. Bureau of Education, 1918), pp. 7, 10, 11.

17 Education Policies Commission, *The Purposes of Education in American Democracy* (Washington, D.C.: Educational Policies Commission, 1938).

1918	1938
Commission for the Reorganization of Education	*Educational Policies Commission— The Purposes of Education in American Democracy*

1918 Commission	1938 Commission
1. Health	1. Self-realization
2. Command of the fundamental process	2. Human relationship
3. Worthy home membership	3. Economic efficiency
4. Vocation	4. Civic responsibility
5. Citizenship	
6. Worthy use of leisure	
7. Ethical character	

A more recent statement for purposes of comparison is the following list set down by the Michigan Department of Education.[18]

1. Michigan education must create an educational environment which fosters the development of mature and responsible citizens.
2. Michigan education must support and advance the principles of democracy by recognizing the worth of every individual and by respecting each person's right to equal participation in the educational process.
3. Michigan education must help each individual acquire a positive attitude toward school and the learning process so that, as a result of his educational experience, he is able to achieve optimum personal growth, to progress in a worthwhile and rewarding manner in the career of his choice, and to render valuable service to society.
4. Michigan education must include adequate provision to assess, evaluate, and improve, on an on-going basis, progress of the educational system in achieving the goals essential for quality education.

The above broad, generalized statements provide an adequate umbrella for more specific educational outcomes. Goals seem to revolve around the learner and his role in society. Clearly, society wants to hold the schools accountable in some measure. Goals are usually general and open to varied definition. More precise statements at state and national levels are probably ill-advised. School systems, responsive to the local community, should articulate goals and objectives that are specifically appropriate to the setting. Once general goals are identified and set forth, procedures for implementation can be initiated. Curriculum development begins with such statements of outcomes, follows through with implementation, and remains dynamic through evaluation. Within recent years many writers in the curriculum field have described the process in what appear to be different ways. In most cases, however, the continuum of ends, means, and evaluation is discernible. Compare the following three plans and schemes for the development of curriculum.

---

[18] Michigan Department of Education, *The Common Goals of Michigan Education* (Lansing: The Michigan Department of Education, 1970), pp. 2–8.

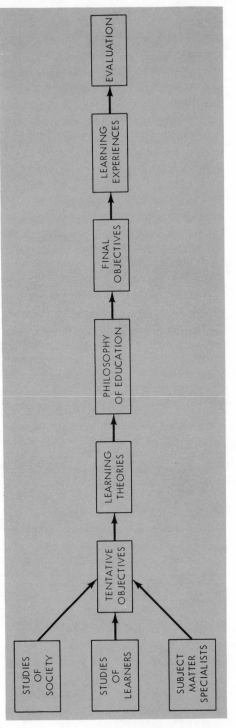

FIGURE 2.1

Taba suggested a seven-phase process as follows:

1. Diagnosis of need,
2. Formulation of objectives,
3. Selection of content,
4. Organization of content,
5. Selection of learning experiences,
6. Organization of learning experiences,
7. Determination of what to evaluate and ways and means of doing it.[19]

In Figure 2.1 Tyler[20] outlines a procedure that is slightly different from Taba's. Tyler would have us pass tentative objectives through philosophical and psychological "screens" before they are finally adopted for implementation through instruction.

A more recent systems design approach has emphasized the feedback

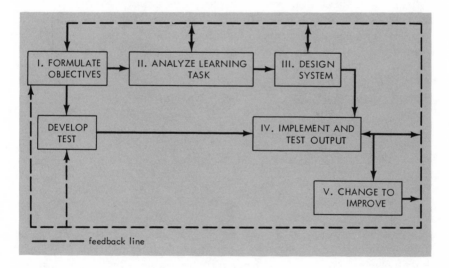

FIGURE 2.2

Bela Banathy, *Instructional Systems* (Palo Alto, Calif.: Fearon Publishers, 1968), p. 28.

[19] Taba, *op. cit.*, p. 12.

[20] Robert Emans, "A Proposed Conceptual Framework for Curriculum Development" in *Contemporary Thought on School Curriculum*, ed. E. C. Short and G. D. Marconnit (Dubuque, Iowa: William C. Brown Company, Publishers, 1969), p. 33.

aspect of the curriculum development process. Figure 2.2 reflects a concern for ongoing evaluation.[21]

Curriculum development is viewed as a pressing need in music education. Precise instructional plans tied to defensible, long-lasting outcomes must be the trademark of music education programs of the future.

PROGRAM BUILDING IN MUSIC

What constitutes the curriculum development or program building process in music? It is a procedure having several phases and begins with a philosophic position which describes the need for music in education of young people.

When a teaching staff has made decisions on the direction that a program of instruction will take, the staff has made a philosophical decision. When precise statements of terminal goals are agreed upon, a possibility of implementation exists. A strong philosophical position will breed statements of terminal goals which in turn serve to generate action patterns to implement the philosophy. There is good reason to support the contention that terminals form a major portion of the philosophic statement. A philosophy of music education provides an ideational framework for curriculum development. Leonhard and House[22] cite three fundamental reasons for the need for a philosophy of music education:

1. A philosophy "serves to guide and give direction to the efforts of the teacher."
2. A sound philosophy "inspires and lightens the work of the music teacher."
3. A philosophy "helps the music teacher clarify and explain the importance of music to his colleagues and to laymen."

For the purpose of the present discussion, the first point in the above rationale will suffice. Decisions on the appropriateness of music learning experiences emerge from philosophic decisions. The most admissible education embraces the basic tenets of aesthetic education. This is simply because that which is unique and fundamental to music is aesthetic. An individual can be led to increased aesthetic sensitivity through the instructional program. Kyme[23] provides an effective definition of aes-

---

21 Banathy, *op. cit.*, p. 28.

22 Charles Leonhard and Robert House, *Foundations and Principles of Music Education* (New York: McGraw-Hill Book Company, 1958), pp. 72–73.

23 George Kyme, "A Study of the Development of Musicality in the Junior High School and the Contribution of Musical Composition to this Development," *Council for Research in Music Education Bulletin* (Summer, 1967), p. 18.

thetic sensitivity as being "dependent upon the capacity to grasp in its completeness and detail a musical idea heard. Accordingly, "knowledge of musical structure design, balance, unity and variety will be reflected in the scores of a test of aesthetic sensitivity." Broudy says the realization of aesthetic value occurs, "whenever we perceive an object as a unified expression of meaningful feeling."[24] The formulation of a statement of philosophical viewpoint provides the springboard for the whole of the curriculum development process. As such it must be arrived by the total music staff by means of cooperative effort.

The program building process is a three-phase operation that provides for its own regeneration. The output of the evaluation phase becomes the input of the ongoing terminal goal determination. The chain is continuous, changeable, and discrete (see Fig. 2.3).

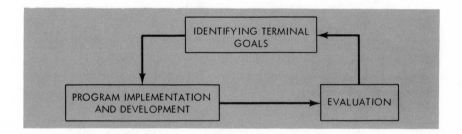

FIGURE 2.3

In outline form each major phase of the process is identified as:

1.0. Identifying terminal goals
      1.1. Bases for goal identification
            1.1.1. Sociological
            1.1.2. Student need
            1.1.3. Subject matter
      1.2. Contributions of research
            1.2.1. Sociological
            1.2.2. Bibliographical
            1.2.3. Philosophical
            1.2.4. Experimental

2.0. Program development and implementation
        2.1. Identifying program objectives and courses
        2.2. Identifying learning topics, tasks, and content

---

[24] Harry Broudy, *Building a Philosophy of Education,* 2nd ed. (Englewood Cliffs, N.J.: Prentice-Hall, Inc., 1961), p. 202.

      2.2.1. Instructional objectives

      2.2.2. Instructional sequence

    2.3. Experience selection and planning

3.0. Evaluation

    3.1. Student evaluation

    3.2. Program evaluation

1.0 IDENTIFYING TERMINAL GOALS

An important part of any curriculum development is identifying terminal goals. Without statements describing human music capability, the music educator is hard put to defend what he is teaching and whether or not it is really important. There is a large audience of skeptics waiting to be convinced. If the results of the instructional program in music are readily discernible in the behavior of graduates, the argument can be easily won. The most successful music programs are those in which the public easily perceives and can evaluate results. Large performance ensembles are distinct examples of easily identifiable results.

1.1 Bases for Goal Identification. Terminal goals in music education should be based on:

1.1.1. The total educational goals of the community and the view local society holds regarding the value of music in education.

1.1.2. The needs of the students for aesthetic expression.

1.1.3. The structure of knowledge derivable from music for decision making about music.

For example, a growing aesthetic awareness and sensitivity are determined to be an important outcome of education in music. Music need not be taught because it produces good citizenship, mental health, or physical stature, for these are not reasonable behaviors as a result of music experiences. In order to grow aesthetically, learners will need to sharpen perceptions of the elements that constitute the art of music. Learners will also need to experience music-making or performance as a personal experience or else they will never be aware of the creative aspect of music. The proper basis for determining goals in music education is the nature of the aesthetic music experience itself and the role of such experience in society.

1.2 Contributions of Research. Several different kinds of research data may make great contributions to the identification of terminal instructional goals. Program building should proceed from a basis other than coffee-break philosophizing. Findings from sociological, bibliographical, and perhaps experimental research are pertinent. Supervisors and teachers must be aware of new developments in the field and alert to current research.

1.2.1 Sociological: The music staff should become well acquainted with the community it serves. What groups make up the population? How are the people employed? Is economic information valuable? Are there special groups with special needs? Who are community leaders? What are prevailing descriptions of music behaviors evident in the community? What are the concert-attending habits of the community? What is the current opinion of the music program? Are there special kinds of initial school music experiences which might be more in line with home background? What is the status of church music support and participation by community members? How can music staff members become more vital musical agents within the community? What kinds of changes would community members like to see in the school music program? What resources or resource people for music learning exist in the community? Can teacher aids be found? How can they best be used? All of the above questions may not apply to any given community. There may be many more appropriate questions. Nevertheless, a well-conceived study of the community with emphasis on its musical culture will be rewarding to the teaching staff. This survey should not confine itself only to things musical. Values, culture, ecology, ethnic populations are only a few variants in communities. Those responsible for school organization and operation should be community conscious at all times. Oliver cites seven key school-community relationships that can provide evidence for needed changes in the school program:[25]

1. How does the community feel about the school? What is being done to improve school-community relations?
2. Has the population of the community changed? If so, in what ways?
3. Does the school have an active PTA or similar organizations?
4. What economic changes have taken place in the community?
5. How much of the time and to whom is the school building open? How is it used?
6. What studies do teachers make of the environmental backgrounds of their students?
7. What community resources are available?

Staff members initiating curriculum reform projects need also be aware of changes within the total society. Do the schools reflect social change? What are important changes in society? What is different in society today as compared to 1950? Are these differences worthy of consideration in designing curriculum?

---

25 Albert I. Oliver, *Curriculum Improvement* (New York: Dodd, Mead & Co., 1965), p. 34.

1.2.2 Bibliographical: The music staff has an obligation to be professionally alert. Supervisors and teachers need to be constantly mindful of innovations in both education and music education. Reports of research found in professional journals and government publications need to be discussed, evaluated, and judged for their usefulness. Programs of study from other schools, communities, and states can provide bases for new programs. Attendance at professional meetings and workshops by members of the staff will provide fuller knowledge of current trends and innovations in music education. It is a function of supervisors to provide in-service programs designed to update teacher competency. A staff should not only know what is new but be able to assess new methodologies and approaches. Serious questions on innovations need answers. Is this new approach appropriate to the program of instruction? Do we have competency to institute such a procedure? Music faculties cannot jump on to bandwagons heedlessly; they must make careful local evaluations of suitability.

1.2.3 Philosophical Research: Before a program of curriculum development can be instituted some philosophical questions must be discussed and subsequently answered. *What are the desired terminal goals for the program of music education?* This inquiry proceeds from individual reading and open discussion among all the staff members. Currently, there are several respected thinkers who carefully describe various points of view regarding aesthetic education (Reimer, 1969; Kaplan, 1967). The music staff needs to become aware of the views expressed by the realist, idealist, or pragmatist in order to forge satisfactory goals for *its* program of music education. The basic goals or outcomes should be stated in precise terms. These statements can provide for evaluation and subsequent analysis of curriculum credibility. To begin the program building process without the terminal goals in sharp focus can bring about confusion, aimlessness, and failure. You cannot build a road if you don't know its final destination.

1.2.4 Experimental: Many forward-looking school systems have instituted programs of research in methodology and the use of various teaching aids. New approaches using home-town subjects are tested. Teachers innovate and experiment. Funds are often available from the administrative offices to underwrite expenses of experimental programs. When the astounding results of the Suzuki instructional programs became apparent, many experimental programs were instituted in schools throughout the United States. Oak Park, Michigan began such a pilot program in one elementary building. Conclusive results brought forth similar programs in other elementary buildings. Another example of experimentation is the opportunity for schools to participate in funded music learning research projects that are being carried out by universities. Another activity in experimental research could be the replication of reported research in order to gauge effectiveness within the local school environment. Care must be exercised before including new procedures in curriculum reform. The feasibility and appropriateness of the innovation must be studied. Very often the process of program building is started by a system-wide curriculum analysis by outside experts. Actually, these studies and surveys form a part of the evaluative phase of curriculum reform. As a rule, these findings generate the awareness of the need for continued redevelopment.

2.0. PROGRAM DEVELOPMENT AND IMPLEMENTATION

The main phase of the program building process is the identification of those learning situations that will bring about desired terminal outcomes. A number of activities are necessary and valuable within this phase: program objectives must be identified, content selected, sequence of instruction proposed, kinds of learning experiences suggested and, finally, day-to-day class planning proposed and initiated.

2.1 Identifying Program Objectives and Courses. Traditionally, music learning is achieved in two kinds of class organization: performance classes and nonperformance classes. The dichotomy is not always clearly seen. Nonperforming classes are often involved in a great deal of music-making. On the other hand, performance classes often include experiences other than skill achievement. Usually, performance classes have as an overall goal skill development but nonperformance courses center on development of knowledge and attitudes.

When a school system is in the process of rebuilding its program of instruction, decisions on the kinds of classes to be offered must be made. Kinds of classes, however, are only a convenience to administrators who need labels for scheduling purposes. The kinds of learning experiences incorporated in music classes are decisions most crucial to the curriculum developer. How will the experiences in each class serve the terminal goals of the music education program? What kinds of learning are appropriate in the given class? How can substantial gains in skills, knowledge, and attitudes be made in each kind of class? What objectives are appropriate in a given class? What objectives are appropriate for such multilevel classes as choruses, orchestras, and bands? Is it reasonable to expect great gains in nonskill learnings in performance classes?

Once the basic framework of the music program is identified by labeling certain courses or classes, appropriate objectives can be prescribed. There will be a general music program in the elementary schools. Program objectives can be identified by year or perhaps by several year blocks as in a nongraded program. A school system organized K–4 and 5–8 might identify program objectives only for each four-year block of music experiences. Whatever seems relevant to an individual system is best. If it is necessary to describe first-grade, second-grade, or third-grade musical objectives, do so. Grouping several years together may facilitate program implementation. There must be precise, accurate program objectives from time to time in order to provide bases for pupil measurement and program evaluation. Almost all school systems provide for beginning instrumental study at approximately age ten. First-year behavioral objectives for such study should then be stated. The same is true for second-year outcomes. Common secondary school course offerings include general music, performing groups, performance training groups, and classes in theory, humanities, and music literature. Objectives appropriate to each class must be stated in precise action terms that allow for assessment and evaluation. Cognitive, affective psychomotor, and perceptual learning can be specifically described in terms of what the student can *do* after instruction.

This phase of curriculum development produces the main building blocks of the music program. Appropriate course objectives will be determined for those classes deemed necessary by the music staff. Expectations of achievement are identified. The attainment of those expectations is more properly within the next phase of program building.

2.2 Identifying Learning Topics, Tasks, and Content. In order to attain program objectives learners need to achieve certain capabilities. As noted, content is selected from the structure of musical knowledge. Content may well include musical elements, musical organization, and musical involvement through performance. Whatever decisions of content may be, they will be based on program objectives produced for each musical experience cluster or class. It is necessary for curriculum developers in music to carefully analyze and define all capabilities needed to achieve given program objectives. These capabilities allow learners to perform at an acceptable level at the end of the class. The precise nature of prerequisite abilities needed for such capabilities is termed task analysis. Curriculum development teams must define carefully all competencies necessary for adequate achievement of a program objective and how they are structured within the learning topic. Mager,[26] Gagné,[27] Yelon,[28] and Banathy[29] have written extensively on the importance of defining learning structures or analyzing tasks. Chapter Four treats the subject in detail. A

---

[26] Mager, *op. cit.*

[27] Robert Gagné, *The Conditions of Learning* (New York: Holt, Rinehart & Winston, Inc., 1970), pp. 172–201.

[28] Yelon, *op. cit.*

[29] Banathy, *op. cit.*

sample structure is also shown in Figure 2.4. As the task is carefully broken down into its components, a learning structure emerges that can help chart instructional sequence.

2.2.1 Instructional Objectives: The total music staff may well be involved with the development of objectives appropriate to instructional program objectives. Individual teachers most involved will bear the brunt of the planning, but total staff participation will provide the most successful base for action. Since program objectives already exist, necessary learning experiences in logical sequence should be identifiable through definition of a series of instructional objectives. Course goals generate behavioral objectives of a subsidiary nature. If, for example, a program objective of scale writing is chosen to be appropriate, what is the learning structure necessary to achieve this goal? All trained musicians can contribute to the development of this structure. There are many approaches.

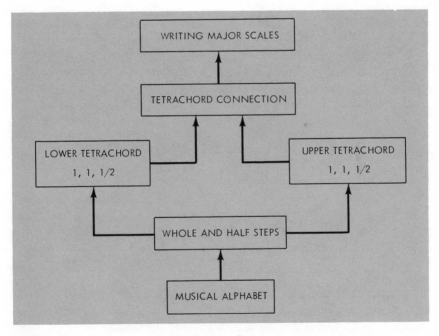

FIGURE 2.4

2.2.2 Instructional Sequence: If patterns of learning achievement are carefully developed, mistakes or skips in the learning continuum can be avoided. Another advantage is the obvious one of learner efficiency. In either case, the key concept is instructional sequence.

A schemata (see Fig. 2.4) can be developed for many music learn-

INSTRUCTIONAL MODULE

Experience Module: (What is the nature of the experience and how will it be
                     conducted?)

Special Materials Required: Titles _____   Number of
                                                             student clock
Film _____   Transparency _____   hours needed
                                                             to complete
Recording _____   Video _____   this module

Musical Hardware _____

_____

INSTRUCTIONAL SETTING

Large Group _____   Small Group _____   Independent _____   Other_____

_____

OBJECTIVE(S):   (Stated in behavior terms, what is this experience designed
                to accomplish?)

Cognitive _____

Affective _____

Psychomotor _____

_____

PREREQUISITES: (What are the most important two or three competencies
                 needed before working on this objective(s)?)

_____

EVALUATION: (What will test whether or not standards of criteria for the
              success of this objective have been reached?)

FIGURE 2.5

ing tasks that are described for program objectives. A glance at the chart will aid in the necessary sequence of things to be learned. The teacher must then plan the kinds of experiences that will produce the desired behaviors at various hierarchical levels of the learning structure. Each program objective will be supported by a number of instructional objectives in turn directly related to learning activities. More detail on this phase of program building will be presented in Chapters Four and Five.

2.3 Experience Selection and Planning. The final stage of the developmental phase is the process of planning day-to-day learning experiences. *It is here that appropriate methodology is chosen.* The degree of exactness in planning reflects the personality of the teacher and the nature of the learning experiences. Some teachers are rigid and require a high degree of exactness in planning. Conversely, a free and easy classroom is more comfortable for others. Discovery learning operates in the latter atmosphere and students became participants in the planning process. In the free creative air of the discovery classroom, objectives are not lost sight of but a gentle, firm hand leads learners into awareness through involvement. No matter at which end of the exactness scale a teacher needs to work, there must be a description of the intent of each learning experience. A convenient form to use in sharply defining these experiences is the experience module (see Fig. 2.5). The module form has several important planning aspects. The experience is identified by level, class, and instructional category. The experience is briefly stated in descriptive terms. Large, small, or independent instructional setting is determined. There is also space for three important statements: (1) The writer must state a behavioral objective and identify it in terms of the kind of learning taking place. (2) The section for prerequisite offers a positive means of achieving instructional sequence. (3) Finally, there is provision for evaluation of achievement of the objectives of the module by means of a recommended technique of assessment.

The advantages of this degree of care in planning are obvious. A complete booklet of modules could represent a course of study, and if musical development on all levels is included, the pattern of musical growth for any given school system will be charted. Teachers will be able to describe average musical behaviors at almost any given point on a maturational continuum.

3.0 EVALUATION

The third phase of program building has been designated a time for evaluation. Actually, two different kinds of evaluation should be taking place—student evaluation and program evaluation.

Evaluation is a process of taking stock and assessing the effectiveness of the program of study. In simple terms, the best way to determine the impact of the program in music education is to measure student behavior in terms of the terminal goals that have been delineated for the program. Measurement alone, however, is not enough. The subsequent analysis of measurement findings constitutes the evaluative process.

3.1 *Student Evaluation.* In each course or class, at certain intervals, measurement of changes in student's knowledges, attitudes, and skills relative to music must be made. There are few tests that can apply to every school situation. It is the responsibility of the teaching staff to construct, try out, and revise measuring instruments for the various curricular offerings.

All measurements and evaluations are first of all made in relation to stated objectives. Objective measures of musical knowledge should be based upon the evaluative sections of experience modules. A part of instructional planning is provision for evaluation. For example, the difficult task of working out means of measuring attitudes and values about music must be broached by the staff. Ways of measuring motor skills against reasonable criteria need development. Psychomotor objectives stated behaviorally are a significant first step. The measurement and subsequent evaluation process is a local responsibility. A few standardized tests are available but it is more valuable to find the means of measuring the objectives decided upon locally than to depend on supposed criterion developed by experts far removed from the teaching situation.

3.2 *Program Evaluation.* On the basis of findings of student measurement, an evaluation of program effectiveness can be initiated. Teaching staffs can become competent in interpreting the results of testing and form a clear picture of what effect curricular experiences may have. On the basis of these evaluations, need for change as well as direction of change may be identified.

As mentioned previously, there is likely to be a time when the objective outsider can help. This evaluator need not always be the college or university expert. Music staff personnel from neighboring communities who work with well-defined instruction programs can also be strong contributors. Nonmusicians, particularly learning system experts, may also be able to assist. If program objectives are well defined, research staffs and measurement experts can aid in evaluating program impact. Nonmusical experts cannot always participate in evaluating musical skills, but they may give new insights in the measurement of skills.

The process thus goes full circle. An organized plan of evaluation constitutes status research of the instructional program. Recommendations based on the findings of such inquiry make up the foundations for future alteration and development of the curriculum. The process begins anew.

TEACHER ROLE IN CURRICULUM DEVELOPMENT

Among other responsibilities of the teaching staff prime importance must be attached to the management of instruction. What does this really mean? It implies competence in decision making on the kinds of learning experiences that are appropriate for learners. There is more. The competent teacher is conscious of the community he serves. He takes time to become familiar with general community activity. More specifically, the music educator assumes the role of a community music agent. He becomes involved in as many ways as possible in musical happenings. He is a humanist and a catalyst. He brings music and people together. The music educator who knows his community and can read its musical pulse will find ways to make the school program more meaningful. His teaching must be relevant to the community he serves. Knowledge of the community will bring about keener awareness of the kinds of students who are the music educator's charge. Teachers are constantly exhorted to know pupils and their needs. This competence doesn't come through classroom contact. What is the student's life like? How does he spend his time? What are current value decisions challenging the student? Does he have musical needs? What are sources of peer pressure? What is current in child-development theory and research?

The teacher must be able to identify the environment in which he is teaching. Students, community, and administration contribute to this environment. Particular emphasis should be placed on working within the administrative structure of the school system. Music educators must be able to describe verbally the need for music in lives of people and the role of music education in humanizing the individual through school experiences in music. Those responsible for school policy should be carefully briefed on music as an educational force.

The music educator should exhibit two competencies. First, he must be a secure musician so that he can identify what is teachable about and with music. Knowledge of subject matter of music and attendant skills provide the base for his musical security. This does not excuse the musical snob who is only able to allow *his* kind of music. Music educators by the very nature of their work need to show tolerance toward all kinds of music. There is involvement with people, and this necessitates the use of "people music"; whatever it might be. Dictatorial music education according to arbitrary teacher taste is not appropriate. On the other hand, teachers should have well-defined musical taste and be prepared to explain sensible reasons for their musical preferences.

The second competency relates to the music educator's role as teacher. A music educator must be comfortable in his role as a teacher. He interacts with students easily, arranges and manipulates the conditions of learning with skill, and facilitates the processes whereby musical behavior is altered.

SUMMARY

The need for renovation of instructional programs was based on flaws in present programs, innovations in the field, and the developing expertise in defining what music education should be. Curriculum development was determined to be a process having three distinct phases: goal identification, development and implementation, and evaluation. Within each phase specific activities were defined and illustrated. Contributions of sociological, philosophical, and experimental research to goal identification were listed. The evaluation phase of program building detailed information and data that allows for the constant readjustment and refinement of the instructional system.

QUESTIONS FOR DISCUSSION AND STUDY

1. Gather data and develop a checklist of musical criteria that can be instrumental in determining when a school music program needs reform.
2. Assemble a number of definitions of aesthetic education that can serve as a springboard for defining terminal behaviors in music education.
3. List needed teacher competencies for successful participation in all phases of curriculum reform.
4. List advantages of the process of program development as suggested in this chapter.
5. List five terminal goals in music education that would accrue from present-day performance experiences.

SUPPLEMENTARY READINGS

Broudy, Harry, *Building a Philosophy of Education* (2nd ed.). Englewood Cliffs, N.J.: Prentice-Hall, Inc., 1961.

Doll, Ronald C., *Curriculum Improvement, Decision Making and Process* (2nd ed.). Boston: Allyn and Bacon, Inc., 1970.

Herrick, Virgil, *Strategies of Curriculum Development*. Columbus, Ohio: C. E. Merrill Books, 1965.

House, Robert, *Curriculum Construction in Music Education, Basic Concepts in Music Education*. Chicago: National Society for the Study of Education, 1958.

Oliver, Albert I., *Curriculum Improvement*. New York: Dodd, Mead & Co., 1965.

Taba, Hilda, *Curriculum Development, Theory and Practice*. New York: Harcourt, Brace & World, Inc., 1962.

Tyler, Ralph, *Basic Principles of Curriculum and Instruction* (Chicago: The University of Chicago Press, 1950.

CHAPTER THREE

determining instructional outcomes

Goals and objectives are descriptions of proposed outcomes of the educational process. The first decision the curriculum builder is faced with is to determine what shall be taught. Goals refer to overall or terminal outcomes but objectives identify year, course, term, or daily instructional aims. Goals and objectives constitute the most important threads in the fabric of the educational process. Although goals describe learner abilities in a general way, objectives relate to specific courses or clusters of experience such as a performance class or a general music class. Objectives are distilled from goal statements and more specifically describe what the learner will be able to do. A single terminal goal might generate a half-dozen objectives for different courses on several levels in the music curriculum.

It should be clear that writing goals and objectives is equivalent in importance to the teaching process itself. Significant teaching is directed toward a specific outcome. It has the purpose of behavioral changes in learners. The direction, extent, and quality of these changes should be known in order to ensure reasonably successful achievement. Objectives generate educational experiences. Decisions that teachers make on classroom activity are based on objectives that are derived from goals. Instructural content leads to the kinds of experiences children will have and is delineated through a series of program and instructional objectives.

Educational literature abounds with words supposedly synonomous with objective. One writer lists the following and implies coincidence of meaning: aims, goals, purposes, outcomes. There really is no universally accepted model phrase. By definition, objectives, aims or goals describe educational outcomes. Some statements relate to courses, others to overall goals. For present purposes, a three-level hierarchical classification will be used: terminal goals, program objectives, and instructional objectives. This classification seems advisable because of the diverse nature of learning experiences in music. The scheme is pictured in Figure 3.1

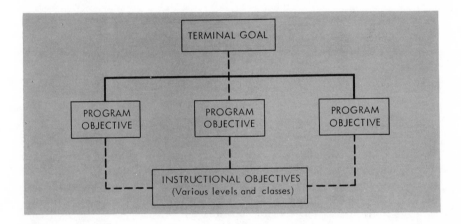

FIGURE 3.1

Terminal Goals. Statements that generally describe learner capabilities upon completing the school music program. Statements of terminal goals need not be overly specific since more than one kind of music class may implement a portion of the goal. Normally, terminal goals are minimal. Each can beget several program objectives. The consequences of program objectives are clusters of instructional objectives common to a single class.

Program Objectives. Statements of a comprehensive nature that specifically describe outcomes of specific music courses or blocks of experiences, e.g., upper-elementary general music, junior-high band, senior-high glee club (see chapter one, p. 11). The following are examples of program objectives that will serve to clarify what is meant by the term. These objectives were proposed by a group of elementary music specialists.

PROGRAM OBJECTIVES FOR THE LOWER ELEMENTARY GRADES

I. Skills

    A. Listening. Given an aural stimulus, the student will be able to:

        1. identify the following kinds of music:
            a. march
            b. program, descriptive
            c. lullaby

        2. identify melodic movement as to up and down, high and low, same and different patterns

        3. differentiate between:
            a. even and uneven rhythmic patterns
            b. beat and rhythmic pattern

        4. identify music in duple, triple pulse divisions and sub-divisions

        5. identify repetition and contrast of rhythmic and melodic phrases

        6. recall a melody after a few hearings

        7. recognize different kinds of performing mediums—chorus, orchestra, band, quartet, electronic

    B. Singing. Given a song by rote, the student will be able to:

        1. sing on pitch within an octave range

        2. sing a two-part round with accuracy

        3. reproduce a simple melodic pattern accurately

        4. use the expressive elements of intensity and tempo changes

    C. Playing: Given a musical stimulus, the student will be able to:

        1. play simple melody instruments and percussion instruments as accompaniments

        2. demonstrate the following concepts using melody and/or percussion instruments:
            a. high, low
            b. loud, soft
            c. slow, fast
            d. play melody and/or percussion instruments

        3. play a melody on the piano by ear

        4. accompany a piece with I, V chords on the Autoharp

    D. Reading. Given a notated melodic excerpt, the student will be able to:

        1. identify and perform even and uneven rhythmic patterns:
            a. two half notes
            b. four quarter notes
            c. four eighth notes
            d. two eighths, quarter note
            e. quarter note, two eights
            f. quarter, eighth, quarter, eighth
            g. quarter rest, quarter note

       h. quarter note, quarter rest

       i. quarter, two eighths, quarter

   2. analyze melodic direction as to steps and skips

   3. identify melodic contour, ascending/descending

II. Creating

A. Composition. Given the dimensions of five pitches, three sound and silence durations, the student is able to:

1. create rhythmic patterns
2. create an accompaniment to a song on rhythm instruments
3. create a melody by singing or playing
4. improvise a melody for a four-line poem by singing or playing
5. create a piece in any available medium

B. Movement. Given a musical stimulus, the student will be able to:

1. fit and imitate rhythmic action of walking, running, marching, skipping
2. demonstrate up, down, high, low by hand and body movement
3. identify form through movement
4. take part in simple dances
5. improvise movements to music
6. identify beat by walking or clapping

III. Attitudes

A. Given free class time and with the availability of library materials—books, recordings, tapes, and instruments—the student makes (and is encouraged to make) some choices concerning his musical preferences and experiences.

B. In composing, improvisation, performing, and listening, students can discover and examine alternatives in solving musical problems.

C. Students can verbalize their musical feelings and perceptions; they are encouraged to articulate what they value musically.

Instructional Objectives. Statements that specifically describe learner capabilities in daily, weekly, or unit achievement.

The differences among the three levels of outcomes can be illustrated as follows:

1. *Terminal goal.* The graduate of the school music program should be able to read musical scores.
2. *Program objective.* Given a piece of music, difficulty similar to "Auld Lang Syne," the eleventh grade high-school music choral student after two tries can sing it at sight (tempo $\quad = 72$). Acceptable performance

would embrace about 90% accuracy in intervals and rhythm. (50 of 57 intervals, 50 of 58 rhythmic placements.)

3. *Instructional objective.* Given a piece of music, nine-year olds can *tap* the rhythm of the melody, difficulty similar to *"Come to the Fair."* Acceptable performance would include 75% accuracy in rhythms (21 of 28) taps correctly placed.

Aside from the obvious age discrepancy, the essential difference between the two objectives is one of comprehensiveness. The second (instructional objective) is only a phase in learner development toward the first, the program objective. Each in turn produces learner capability that is generally defined in the terminal goal. This three-level hierarchy of outcomes is favored because once a teacher is given terminal goals, he can identify instructional and program objectives for his piece of the music education program. There can be unity of purpose even though class experiences vary. Goals are general and not limiting in nature, while objectives are precise statements that describe observable levels of student behavior as a result of instruction.

IDENTIFYING TERMINAL GOALS

Music education can be defined as a process by which human musical behavior is more or less permanently altered. Almost all goals for music education should be identified in relation to behaviors consistent with music involvement (activity). People function with music in four primary ways: pure perception of sound, knowledge of verbal labels for sounds and symbols, physically manipulating their bodies in meaningful performance, and indulging in nonverbal feelingful or emotional responses. Educational psychologists label the latter three of these interactions as cognitive, psychomotor, and affective operations.

Perception is a unique process in the musical experience, i.e., acting on nonverbal, tonal, sound stimuli. Perception, however, turns immediately into a cognitive or affective operation. People either just relax and enjoy great quantities of sound or they initiate a series of mental operations that can be classified as cognitive behavior. A separate classification of perceptual outcomes in instruction is probably unwarranted at this time.

For our present purposes, the foregoing categories of musical involvement will be used as a goal identification. The system simply will help classify musical learning outcomes more clearly. Primary terminal goals for music education should be categorized in the classifications noted. Certainly there are for some teachers identifiable goals that are nonmusical in nature (citizenship, mental health, mental discipline). As terminal goals, these must be secondary because they are not unique to music learning experience. Students may very well learn or achieve these goals more efficiently in other classes. Terminal music goals must be developed by every school music staff. For each kind of music/people interaction, consider the following:

I. AFFECTIVE

Affective goals are those that identify feelingful, emotional, or attitudinal operations with music. For the most part, they are nonobservable, but evidence of occurrence may be obtained by observation of action and in some cases by verbal description. A group of writers who were responsible for focusing attention on affective goals and objectives in education define these outcomes as those "which emphasize feeling tone, an emotion or a degree of acceptance or rejection."[1] These goals pinpoint student interests, appreciations, attitudes, prejudices, and values as alterable educational targets.

The graduate of the school music program:
1. exhibits tolerance to many kinds of music;
2. can utilize a scale of musical values for determining his taste spectrum (the scale is based on musical criteria);
3. is sufficiently self-motivated to participate in home and community music activities;
4. seeks active or vicarious music involvement for himself;
5. displays values for musical quality in performance and/or listening diet.

II. COGNITIVE

Terminal cognitive goals in music education will include the mental manipulation of aural and visual musical phenomena. It is convenient to separate cognitive activity in music into perceptual and conceptual/verbal operations. This division makes possible precise differentiation between pure awareness of sound and mental operations associated with musical cognition. Terminal cognitive goals in music education might include:

---

[1] Benjamin S. Bloom, ed., *Taxonomy of Education Objectives, Affective Domain Handbook II* (New York: David McKay Co., Inc., 1964), p. 7.

The graduate of the school music program:

1. can recall specific musical compositions;
2. can perceive, sort, classify, and react to pulse, timbre, form, style, volume, and pitch;
3. can verbalize and/or manipulate facts regarding musical symbols and terminology;
4. can possess a working knowledge of important historical, traditional, or cultural significance of all kinds of music.

III. Psychomotor

Terminal goals of a psychomotor nature reflect the acquisition of music performance skills. Clearly, music educators have been successful in achieving psychomotor goals through the various performance classes common to the American high school. Very often these outcomes are thought to be more valuable than any other goals associated with musical learning. Furthermore, performance skill is easy to observe and thus satisfies the behaviorists' demand for observable acts to document learning gains. For the nonperformance class student, certain manipulative skill goals are equally worthy. The following examples include actual operational goals from several school systems:

The graduate of the school music program:

1. can exhibit performance skills appropriate to his capacity which reflect cognitive and affective awareness in music;
2. can perform (at least on the enjoyment level) a musical instrument (including voice);
3. can demonstrate musical information through learned physical movement, either in bodily motion or refined, skilled performance.

All the foregoing goals (affective, cognitive, and psychomotor) are purposely general and lack definition. Goals are necessary because they generate program and instructional objectives. They give direction to the instructional program and illustrate the need for more precision in stating what the learner will attain. Classes, units, and daily experiences with music need to have precise direction toward something. Carefully stating objectives is the next step in developing the school music curriculum.

WHY OBJECTIVES?

Selecting and stating precise objectives offer the teacher a number of advantages. Since well-defined objectives are difficult to produce, the advantage should be clear before investing time and energy in their development. Herrick identifies the following five functions of objectives as crucial:[2]

1. Objectives define the direction of educational development.
2. Objectives help select desirable learning experiences.
3. Objectives help define the scope of an educational program.
4. Objectives help define the emphasis to be made in an educational program.
5. Objectives form one of the major basis for evaluation.

For example, as an evaluation base objectives function as guidelines for measurement and student assessment. Some school systems use objectives as a basis for communicating student progress to parents. The following report card using objectives is being used in one Michigan school system.

First- and Second-grade music—objectives and evaluation for ＿＿＿＿＿＿ School System, Michigan.[3]
1. Can clap a steady beat while the teacher plays a song on the piano ＿＿.
2. Can clap the rhythm of a song the teacher is singing ＿＿＿＿＿＿.
3. Can clap the rhythm of a familiar song along ＿＿＿＿＿＿＿.
4. Can clap the rhythm of a familiar song while someone claps the beat ＿＿.
5. Can clap the beat of a familiar song while someone claps the rhythm ＿＿.
6. Can identify whether or not the teacher is clapping the beat or rhythm of the song ＿＿＿＿＿＿＿＿＿＿.
7. Can sing in tune ＿＿＿＿＿＿＿＿＿＿.
8. Can hear the difference between walking, running, skipping and galloping music ＿＿＿＿＿＿＿＿＿.
   (The child shows he knows by doing the activity appropriate to the music played by the teacher.)
9. Can strum the Autoharp with a steady beat while the class sings a song ＿＿.
10. Can clap while the teacher plays the beat ＿＿＿＿＿＿＿＿.
11. Can clap combination of ＿＿＿＿＿＿＿＿＿.

The teacher merely checks which objectives have been met by each student and dates achievement.

Good objectives also provide a reasonable basis for test construction. Consider the following:

---

[2] Virgil Herrick, *Strategies of Curriculum Development*, eds. James B. McDonald, Don W. Anderson, and Frank B. May (Columbus, Ohio: Charles E. Merrill Books, Inc., 1965), p. 89.

[3] Special Project Committee of M.M.E.A., *I-O Newsletter*, Vol. I, No. 2 (May, 1970), p. 3.

By the end of the sixth grade, the learner should be able to identify four out of five aurally dictated rhythmic patterns from a set of given notated rhythmic patterns.

The implication for testing is clear; five examples are dictated either by teacher dictation or taped stimulus. The learner will choose from an undetermined number of responses as if he were taking a multiple-choice test.

Clearly stated objectives also aid in sequencing instruction in a reasonable form. Once a teacher has developed a set of program objectives for a specific segment of the curriculum, daily instructional objectives can be generated in order to bring the learner to acceptable performance levels for program objectives. During the development process, the teacher can make decisions on sequence of experience. It will be a carefully decided sequence and will make the learning and teaching process more efficient because outcomes are clearly identified.

THE QUALITIES OF AN OBJECTIVE

An objective has several qualities that must be considered before one attempts to write. Chief among these qualities is exactness of communication. Precise statements of instructional intent tell people interested in the educational process what we are doing and what we hope to accomplish. A well-stated objective is a communication to students, other teachers, administrators, and parents. The quality of the communication is crucial. According to Mager, "the best statement is the one that excludes the greatest number of possible alternatives."[4] The words used in an objective must describe precisely what the learner will be able to do, how well he will be able to do it, and under what conditions he will have to do it. When writing an objective, it is necessary to choose unambiguous words, words which also are in the vocabulary of the individual to whom the objective is addressed. The capability described in the objective must be translated into words familiar to the learner. Without this level of accuracy, communication will not exist.

Music educators are often guilty of vague descriptions of what learners should be able to do after music instruction. There is an angelic glow related to the intents and benefits of music learning just because it is an art. Students are said to appreciate, value, prize, or know music. At times, music educators will state that learners "will enjoy" or "know the inherent value of music." Although lofty sounding, these statements do not

---

[4] Robert F. Mager, *Preparing Instructional Objectives* (Palo Alto: Fearon Publishers, 1962), p. 10.

constitute admissible objectives for music education but are more in the nature of terminal goals. Their communicative power is almost meaningless. For example, what meaning does the following have? *At the conclusion of a school general music class the learner will enjoy music.* Among others, the problem word is enjoy. What constitutes enjoyment? Twenty music educators could give twenty separate interpretations of this objective. Following are some possible interpretations of the word "enjoy":

1. has a good time with music;
2. sings loud on the good old hymn-tunes in church;
3. chooses music as a leisure time activity;
4. purchases any recording for background listening;
5. has *Muzak* piped into his home.

Many more interpretations are possible. The problem is not the rightness or the wrongness of any one of these meanings. The word "enjoy" is so vague in its meaning that as a communicator it is virtually useless. The following list of verbs contains examples of nonspecific action that are open to more than one interpretation. This list and those that follow are based on similar material found in *Preparing Instructional Objectives* by R. F. Mager. By and large, the objective writer should avoid these:

Verbs that are too broad:

Respond	Generate	Observe	Know	Have faith in
Do	Deduce	Test	Understand	Love
Perform	Infer	Apply	Appreciate	Cherish
Use	Examine	Interpret	Believe	Value

On the other hand, the following list of verbs is more acceptable because of the accuracy of activity implied:

Count	List	Draw	Name	Regroup
Select	Alphabetize	Construct	Recall	Tabulate
Choose	Arrange	Rename	Recite	Sing
Pick out	Classify	Complete	Describe	Play
Identify	Label	Tap	Match	Move to
Delete	Measure	State	Convert	Clap

To the first list a number of vague words common to music activity could be added. Phrases similar to "to love music," "artistic performance," "to interpret," "very musical" are problems for objective writers in music education. People who appreciate music behave differently from those who do not. Music educators need to identify carefully behavioral differences and use these statements as a basis for program and instructional objectives. It is possible to include the word appreciate or enjoy in an objective, but not without a qualifying phrase. For example, a learner exhibits appreciation of music by attending and writing careful descriptions of ten community concerts. This statement includes a workable definition of appreciation. Anyone reading the statement would know precisely what the learner will do to show that he appreciates.

Perhaps the most stringent test of the communicability of an objective would be in the educational practice. Suppose that a general music teacher very carefully listed program objectives in precise terms. If another teacher can achieve the acceptable behavior levels as indicated, there would clearly be communication of instructional intent. A high level of objective writing behavior is certainly evident in the first teacher.

Objectives must also communicate to learners. Education is a process of changing behaviors. If a student is aware of what change is desired and to what degree, he is more likely to succeed. If he is supposed to know a quantity of information, how is he to display the knowledge? By performing, writing, tabulating, or what? The exact terms of acceptable performance must be a part of the communication.

Two other lists of verbs should be identified; those that are too specific and those that need further definition if the objective is to communicate. The first list identifies test-taking behavior and the words are unrelated to a real-life situation:

Verbs that are too specific

Check	Put an X on	Write the number of
Circle	Draw a ring around	Write the letter of
Underline	Put a mark on	Draw a line between
Shade	Color the same as . . .	Put a box around

The toss-up verb needs precise delineation of the activity required:

Toss-up verbs (probably need to be further defined in the objective)

Demonstrate	Collect and synthesize	Contrast
Discriminate	Determine	Predict
Differentiate	Answer	Locate
Distinguish	Compare	Give

TERMINAL BEHAVIOR DEFINED

The second important quality of a program or instructional objective is the precision with which it describes the terminal behavior being sought. Mager defines terminal behavior as "the behavior you would like your learner to be able to demonstrate at the time your influence over him ends."[5] Students, teachers, interested lay public, and administrators should all be able to interpret what capability is the object of instruction.

Some program objectives in music education will describe behaviors unrelated to music performance; others will be solely description of music skills. Actually, objectives will relate to three kinds of music learning: cognition (including perception), affective, and psychomotor. These categories have been identified as behavioral areas in music. Statements like "buys records," "goes to concerts," "registers for a music appreciation course" might typify some program objectives at the conclusion of junior-high general music. Certainly many program objectives would include phrases relating to attitudes, appreciations, and values of music. All objectives are best determined by local music education staffs, who should select objectives appropriate to their teaching environment and special student needs.

Performance objectives might include statements similar to "given a piece of music, the learner can play or sing." This kind of program or instructional objective would also specify whether performance was with or without an instrument. Objectives describing musical knowledge might call for the student to list, recite orally, or to recall names of musical compositions. Each kind of objective would ask for behaviors appropriate to the kind of learning represented: attitude, knowledge, skill, or perception. According to Mager, there are several important questions to ask when framing statements of program objectives. He includes the following:[6]

1. What will the learner be provided?
2. What will the learner be denied?
3. What are the conditions under which you will expect the terminal behavior to occur?
4. Are there any skills that you are specifically not trying to develop? Does the objective exclude such skills?

All of these questions will aid one who is attempting to define program objectives. Consider, for example, the following program objective for a high-school general music appreciation course:

Given a three-part musical composition, the student can identify the main elements of the form after one listening.

---

5 *Ibid.,* p. 2.
6 *Ibid.,* p. 27.

The objective clearly communicates what the learner will have to work with. Compositions other than three-part forms are not included. The conditions under which the behavior is to be observed are only partially stated. It is clear that the learner will perform an identification activity after hearing a recording one time. The exact nature of what he will be doing is not clear. The objective may be rewritten with greater precision as follows:

> Given a three-part musical composition, the learner can mark the conductor's score where the main thematic elements occur. This activity is expected after one practice listening.

Here the objective communicates to the learner exactly what is expected. He will know that in order to reach the objective, he will hear a piece of music and be called upon to mark the score in order to identify thematic materials.

PERFORMANCE CRITERIA

The final dimension of an objective is the criterion that will determine a successful level of learner achievement. Specification of an acceptable level of performance on a given objective is one of the important contributions the skilled teacher can make in curriculum development. Naturally, the determination of minimum acceptability is arbitrary in nature. Inexperienced teachers are likely to set unreasonable levels. A combined staff effort at curriculum building will bring together experienced teachers and beginners and should produce rational levels of performance. According to Mager,[7]

> If you can specify at least the minimum acceptable performance for each objective, you will have a performance standard against which to test your instructional program; you will have a means for determining whether your programs are successful in achieving your instruction intent.

To illustrate, study the following program objective developed by the instrumental music staff at West Ottawa Public Schools, Holland, Michigan:

> *Program Objective for Three-Year Middle School Grade 8—Instrumental Music*
>
> Given eight printed melodic excerpts, eight measures in length, the learner will perform, at sight, all on his instrument with no more than two mistakes per excerpt. A mistake is de-

---

[7] *Ibid.,* p. 44.

fined as an error in pitch, time, articulation or interpretation. The error unit will be the measure allowing a maximum eight errors per excerpt. The following dimensions of musical information will be in effect.

A. Note and rest values   ▬ ▬ ▬ ⸙ 𝄾 𝄾

o, ♩., ♩, ♪, ♪, ♪

B. Meters— $\frac{2}{4}$ $\frac{3}{4}$ $\frac{4}{4}$ $\frac{6}{8}$

C. Articulation—staccato, legato, slur

D. Dynamics—pp, p, mp, mf, f, ff

E. Tempo—76–120 beats per minute

The learner will be given two attempts at each excerpt at a tempo established by the instructor.

SOME SAMPLE OBJECTIVES

The objectives listed in Table 3.1 accurately define expected behaviors. These objectives were developed for a course on the college freshman level and were aimed at acquainting future elementary teachers with music. These statements particularly refer to perception behaviors generated with self-instructional listening materials. Although, according to the hierarchy, they are program objectives they must also serve as terminal since many of the students will take only one music course. Some of the objectives are achieved in small group instruction, others in individualized training. They are included only to serve as examples; there is no intention to indicate primacy or philosophical value. The identification of objectives is a local staff responsibility and function.

EVALUATING OBJECTIVES

Second in importance to the actual writing of an instructional or program objective is the evaluation of the objective. Music instructional staffs engaged in the process of defining objectives should develop appropriate criteria for judging each objective before, during, and after it is functioning in the learning system. One list of evaluative criteria for objectives has been provided by Banathy.[8]

---

[8] Bela Banathy, *Instructional Systems* (Palo Alto: Fearon Publishers, 1968), pp. 34–35.

Table 3.1 Sample Objectives from an Introductory Music Course

Element	Conditions and Behavior	Acceptable Performance Level
A. SOUND QUALITY		
1. Timbre	Discriminating between two or among three sound sources to include the following:	
	Families woodwind, brass, strings, percussion	By family, eight out of ten responses correct.
	Instruments flute, oboe, clarinet, bassoon, saxophone, cornet, horn, trombone, tuba, violin, cello, bass viol, snare drum, xylophone, bass drum, cymbals, tympani	By individual instrument five out of ten responses correct.
2. Intensity	Differentiating between paired sound levels and gradations of level using the following list of musical symbols: pp p mf f ff crescendo dimuendo	By level, eight out of ten correct responses. By gradations, ten out of ten responses correct.
3. Articulation	Identifying the following performance techniques using the appropriate terminology: roll, staccato, legato, tremolo, pizzicato, glissando, sforzando.	Eight out of ten responses correct.
B. RHYTHM		
1. Beat	Tabulating the total number of pulses during a period of time. This capability is also appropriate during a period of silence.	Tabulation should be 90% accurate, e.g., plus or minus one where ten is correct.

Table 3.1 (cont.)

Element	Conditions and Behavior	Acceptable Performance Level
2. Accent	Tabulating the emphasized pulses during a period of time up to twenty seconds. This capability is also appropriate during a like period of silence.	Tabulation should be 90% accurate.
3. Meter	Discriminating among two, three, or five pulse groupings.	Nine out of ten responses correct.
4. Tempo	Differentiating between paired rates of speed and graduations of speed levels using the following list of terminology: lento, andante, allegro, presto, ritard accelerando.	Seven out of ten responses correct.
5. Pattern	Differentiating between paired rhythm patterns—same/different. Values—eighth, quarter, half, and rests.	Four out of five responses correct.
	Identifying the aural with the visual representation—values the same as the first part.	Two out of five responses correct.
6. Syncopation	Identifying the aural with the visual among multiple choices. Examples to include only eighth, quarter, eighth in 2/4, 3/4 or 4/4 meters.	Two out of five responses correct.
7. Varied Meters	Differentiating and identifying meter changes of paired or repeated examples: duple simple, duple compound, triple simple.	Two out of five responses correct.
C. MELODY		
1. Direction	Labeling the contour of melody as uni- or multi-directional.	Eight out of ten responses correct.
2. Register	Identifying melody placement or tessitura by comparing paired examples as follows: very high, high, medium, low, very low.	Three out of four responses correct.

Table 3.1 (cont.)

Element	Conditions and Behavior	Acceptable Performance Level
3. Step and Leap	Discriminating between conjunct and disjunct melodic motion.	Five out of ten responses correct.
4. Major/Minor	Identifying each example as major or minor melody.	Eight out of ten responses correct.
5. Polyphony	Tabulating the number of melodic lines, e.g., the number of entrances in a fugue.	Tabulation plus or minus one of actual number.
D. HARMONY		
1. Construction	Verbally describing the three intervals used in each of the following triads: major, minor, diminished, augmented.	Nine out of twelve responses correct.
2. Quality	Differentiating paired examples as being consonant or dissonant chords. Identifying major/minor triads in any position.	Six out of ten responses correct. Three out of five responses correct.
3. Cadence	Identifying the cadence as V–I, IV–I, V_7–I, V_7–VI, I–V.	Two out of five responses correct.
4. Tonal/Atonal	Labeling examples as tonal or atonal.	Three out of five responses correct.
5. Modulation	Tabulating the number of modulations (cadence confirmation is definition).	Plus or minus two of actual number.

1. How does this objective describe what is expected?
   a. Does it use verbs denoting observable action?
   b. Does it indicate the stimulus that is to evoke the expected behavior?
   c. Does it specify resources to be used and the persons to interact?
2. How does the objective state how well the behavior is expected to be performed?
3. How does the objective state the circumstances under which the learner is expected to perform?

Another writer notes the following criteria for evaluating objectives. Each of the four main parts of the objective should be a part of the evaluation: who, what, when, and how much—who performs, what he does, when he does it, and how much is satisfactory.

Well-written objectives will not take the place of a good teacher, but they will serve to sharpen the efficiency of the learning process if the learner can be apprised of what is to happen. Students are more likely to arrive at the right place if they know where they are going.

SUMMARY

The most important considerations regarding a well-constructed objective were accurate communication, definition of the terminal behavior sought, conditions of observation, and acceptable criteria level. Hazards of preparing objectives for each kind of music learning were noted. Some of the appropriate criteria for evaluating an objective were presented.

1. An objective is a statement of teacher intent describing what the student will be doing to show his mastery of the objective.
2. To be worthwhile, an objective must:
   A. specify a change that is observable;
   B. be attainable; i.e., both the learner and the teacher must be able to control the conditions to achieve this change;
   C. be relevant; i.e., both the learner and the teacher must have a commitment to achieve this change.
3. To be behavioral, an objective statement must:
   A. specify observable, measurable, terminal behavior;
   B. specify conditions under which behavior will be evaluated;
   C. specify criterion—minimum level or acceptable performance.
4. An objective is intended to communicate, and, therefore, must be unambiguous and concise.
5. A behavioral objective must be relevant to a student's beyond-school behavior.

The value of describing goals and objectives in music education was identified. A three-level system of specifying educational outcomes was employed: terminal goals, program objectives, and instructional objectives.

QUESTIONS FOR STUDY AND DISCUSSION

1. List criteria important to developing good instructional objectives.
2. Write an appropriate objective for a specific kind and level of music instruction.
3. List a half-dozen terminal performance behaviors for instrumental players.
4. Collect and evaluate objectives from school instructional programs.
5. List what you believe to be the objectives of the course for which you are using this book.

SUPPLEMENTARY READINGS

Banathy, Bela, *Instructional Systems*. Palo Alto: Fearon Publishers, 1968.

Gagné, Robert M., "Educational Objectives and Human Performance" in *Learning and the Educational Process*, ed. J. D. Krumboltz. Chicago: Rand McNally & Co., 1965.

Kibler, Robert, Larry L. Barker, and D. T. Miles, *Behavioral Objectives and Instruction*. Boston: Allyn and Bacon, Inc., 1970).

Leonhard, Charles, and Robert House, *Foundations and Principles of Music Education* (2nd ed.). New York: McGraw-Hill Book Company, 1972.

Mager, Robert F., *Preparing Instructional Objectives*. Palo Alto: Fearon Publishers, 1962.

Popham, J. L., and Eva Baker, *Determining Instructional Goals*. Englewood Cliffs, N.J.: Prentice-Hall, Inc., 1970.

CHAPTER
FOUR

the content
of instruction

Music is unique among the areas
of study available to students. It offers socially valued behavior with nonverbal material—learning achievement not tied to the students' general
academic and reading ability. In like manner, music offers a vehicle of
self-expression that finds peer approval. Music learning experiences can
afford students the opportunity to create and recreate in the most personal way even though they are associated with a group. Most important,
the study of music allows the learner to become involved with recognized
works of art and develop awareness of the aesthetic essence of these objects. As he grows in aesthetic awareness, the student gains in his ability
to value art objects for their intrinsic worth. He perceives the elements
of construction and organization and is able to create a musical value
system of his own. The possibility of accepting great musical art is an
important part of his existence and the realization of the human endeavor in music can become a part of his conscious existence. Music study
can then make a difference in the quality of human existence.

In another way music is a unique area of study because of the very
nature of the discipline. There is need for skill development that is basi-

cally psychomotor. A strong body of knowledge that embraces the nomen-
clature and tradition of music is important for purposes of increased
intellectual involvement. Music learning leads to valuing musical art as
an integral part of life. Finally, and most basically, all music experiences
are dependent on aural perceptions that provide for many learners a
unique way to receive important stimuli.

If it is to be meaningful, instruction in music must satisfy the following criteria that identify the parameters of the music experience:

1. *Music is an aural art.* Music is a phenomenon that is experienced
   through the ear. One does not look at music, feel music, taste music, or
   smell music. We hear music and, therefore, the basis of all instructional
   programs in music must be the cultivation of an acute musical ear.
   This is a simple but often overlooked truth that must be the cornerstone of all music learning.
2. *A learned musician thinks tonally.* Once a basis for aural perception is
   developed, students of music must develop a sense of melodic, harmonic, and rhythmic imagery. Thought processes must be in terms of
   musical ideas, sounds, and the collective notions of tonal phenomena.
3. *Music provides a means of self-expression.* Music is a different means
   of expressing something human. Substituting sounds in time for various
   verbal forms of communication offers a unique vehicle for expressing
   innermost human feeling and experience.
4. *Music is realized through performance.* The most complete means of
   grasping the full significance of the musical experience is to become
   music. An individual can only do this as a performer regardless of how
   humble the level. It is not possible to gain joy from singing vicariously.
   If it were possible, there would be no need for singing.
5. *Music is a cultural artifact.* From the sociological point of view music
   is one of many phenomena produced by men that gives specific dimension to the society that has been created. It is an expression of the
   human condition, found in all societies and dedicated to eclipse the
   poor confusion of verbal designation.

In the final analysis, decision regarding content should be made
with the nature of musical art clearly in mind. Content will generate
experiences; experiences will be the means of musical growth and development.

THE PROBLEM OF CONTENT

There is no shortage of pursuable goals and objectives for music
education. Given time, any music teaching staff can identify a host of
worthy aims for music instruction. Once objectives have been assembled,

the music staff is left to determine how the objectives should be implemented. Six criteria for identifying content have been identified by Taba:[1]

1. Validity and significance,
2. Consistency with social realities,
3. Balance of breadth and depth,
4. Provision for wide range of objectives,
5. Learnability and adaptability to experiences of students,
6. Appropriateness to the needs and interests of students.

In addition, because of the specialized areas of instruction in music, a seventh is necessary:

7. Music content will be dependent on facilities, equipment, and staff capability.

1. VALIDITY AND SIGNIFICANCE OF MUSIC CONTENT

Instructional content in music should include material and experiences that permit efficiency in student learning. Instructional time is precious and trivial, nonmusical objectives can dictate content that is clearly not germane to the central goals of music education. Content must reflect that for which the student is to be held accountable. Given specific objectives, content should embrace those things which can assure student achievement. Decisions on whether or not there are validity and significance in the instructional program must be made in the light of the philosophical view expressed by the staff through the terminal goals and program objectives. Constant evaluation of what is going on in the classroom leads to a careful appraisal of how instructional content is being realized. The most important question to answer is, "What must the student master in order to solve the musical problems important to him?" There will be as many answers as there are different kinds of instructional programs in music. Teachers should be thinking about what must be deleted or added. Unfortunately, it is often in the nature of curriculum development that more is constantly added but little taken away or restructured. If something new is to be added to the curriculum, it may be well to investigate what kinds of classes could absorb new objectives by deleting some content no longer useful. The watchword is efficiency in instruction; efficiency should be a primary obligation for everyone associated with the instructional planning process.

---

[1] Hilda Taba, *Curriculum Development, Theory and Practice* (New York: Harcourt, Brace & World, Inc., 1962), pp. 267–89.

2. THE CONTENT OF THE MUSIC PROGRAM SHOULD BE CONSISTENT WITH THE SOCIETY IN WHICH IT RESIDES

It is totally unrealistic for program builders in music to ignore the social and cultural milieu the music program is to serve. The content of instruction can and should vary immensely according to the community. There is an essential basic body of information for coping effectively with any musical stimuli. Learners must acquire certain skills, knowledge, and experiences before they can be truly independent in making decisions on music and in solving musical problems. Each staff member can decide what constitutes this body of central knowledge and carefully delineate content in keeping with social realities. The music staff should be aware of the community and equip programs with more than token reference to the society being served.

3. THE CONTENT OF THE MUSIC PROGRAM SHOULD PROVIDE FOR BREADTH AND DEPTH OF STUDY

An instructional program in music should provide opportunities for all children to find self-expression through music. A wide range of learning experiences can allow for both talented and less gifted children to realize their music potential. Similarly, those who have the motivation for great individual skill development should have the opportunity through performance classes of many kinds (large and small ensembles as well as solo work). Music staffs who offer a wide spectrum of musical experiences in the curriculum can effectively meet the diffuse nature of differences in individual musical capacity. For example, Western art music is not the only vehicle for self-expression in music. Formal and informal performance activities that incorporate great differences in the kinds of learning materials used should be offered. Music program planners should also recall that music learning experiences can include a variety of activities but basically embrace *creating, performing,* and *listening.*

4. THE MUSIC EDUCATION PROGRAM SHOULD PROVIDE CONTENT THAT EMBRACES A WIDE RANGE OF OBJECTIVES

The identification of cognitive, perceptual, affective, and motor skill objectives should provide for instructional content that brings about a total kind of musical growth in children. Children confront music through the curriculum. The kinds of experiences facilitating this confrontation should result in expanding knowledge about music, increasing awareness of musical events during listening, sharpened motor skills, and growing desire to include music as a valued life activity. It is appropriate to remember that learning experiences in music may very well serve more than one objective. Performance classes are usually thought of as skill development laboratories but other objectives and goals may be successfully pursued. For example, life-long attitudes toward music involvement are developed in performance classes. Conductor/teachers ought to plan for learning experiences that include the broadest range of content.

5. THE CONTENT OF THE MUSIC PROGRAM
SHOULD BE REFLECTED IN EXPERIENCES
THAT PROVIDE FOR DIFFERENCES AMONG STUDENTS

Learning experiences should be designed so that pupils can experience success. Program builders must take into account the developmental stages for which instruction is designed. Teachers often have a tendency to overestimate student capability during the identification of objectives phase of curriculum development. Program objectives may sound good and look good but be truly unrealistic. Provision for ongoing evaluation and analysis of classroom activity can result in reshaping instructional patterns to better fit student capability. The wise teaching staff carefully assesses beginning abilities of learners for specific classes. On the other hand, it is not sensible to teach what children already know. Prerequisites can be identified so that students will be involved in the most appropriate and efficient learning sequence. A program of preassessment is essential to efficient content organization.

6. THE CONTENT OF THE MUSIC PROGRAM SHOULD REFLECT
THE NEEDS AND INTERESTS OF THE STUDENTS

Much has been written about beginning instruction with what the students know and can do. A strong program of measurement and evaluation of student abilities, interests, desires, and needs is the logical means to acquire information about the pupils to be served by any instructional system. This evaluation process is continuous because student capabilities change as a result of our dynamic society. Measurement techniques for acquiring information about students are becoming more refined all the time. It is now possible to obtain substantially reliable information on the student's previous music achievement and latent music ability. Similarly, new measures of attitude and taste are constantly being reported in the professional literature of music education. Well-informed music staffs can take advantage of these developments and come closer to building an instructional program in keeping with student interests. Moreover, individual teachers can practice guided cooperative planning with students and forge more relevant instructional programs.

7. THE CONTENT OF THE MUSIC EDUCATION PROGRAM IS APPROPRIATE TO PHYSICAL AND STAFF CAPABILITIES

A great deal of expensive specialized instructional equipment is needed to implement a broad music program. If there is to be individualized instruction for learners, the equipment should be readily available. It is foolish to design learning experiences for which proper equipment is not at hand. In the same vein, classes for which there is no well-qualified teacher are best forgotten. For example, there is no need to think about an allied arts or humanities course unless a staff member who has the interest and motivation to participate in an instructional team can be released. Realistic planning for instruction must take into account the kinds of equipment available, the physical limitations of space, and the particular capabilities of teachers. Music staffs must plan a program that is realistic to the situation and avoid visionary proposals designed to please administrators and school boards. A curriculum must be developed to earn the support of the public through proven accountability.

Other curriculum specialists have written extensively on the content of curriculum. For example, Smith, Stanley, and Shores[2] proposed four different methods of determining the content of instruction:

1. *Judgmental procedure.* The music staff meets and decides what shall constitute the content of instruction. The decisions are arbitrary but reflect, at least, superficial consensus of the staff.

2. *Experimental procedure.* After developing minilearning sequences for a variety of levels and classes, the packages are put into the instructional program. Action research procedures determine the effectiveness of package to bring students to identified criteria levels.

3. *Analytical procedure.* Decisions about instructional content are arrived at by closely examining what the educated musician or musical person can do. Goals are distilled from this which in turn bring about instructional and program objectives.

4. *Consensual procedure.* The music staff engages in a descriptive research study that collects data regarding what a wide sample of music educators believe to be important in music education. Data are collated and com-

---

[2] B. O. Smith, W. O. Stanley, and J. H. Shores, *Fundamentals of Curriculum Development,* rev. ed. (Yonkers-on-Hudson, N.Y.: World Book Company, 1957), pp. 152–67.

pared to existent programs. Suggested changes in emphasis are identified and implemented through the program building process.

In any event, music staffs must initially decide what they wish a graduate of their school system to be. A number of questions need clear, communicative answers. For example, what kinds of terminal goals are appropriate for music education? What are reasonable expectations of student behaviors after they have completed a normal thirteen-year course of study in music? Statements of expected outcomes must be the products of concerted efforts of the local music staffs. It is reasonable to suppose that terminal goals will vary from system to system. Teachers teach best those things they believe in most. The accomplishment of goals cannot be expected of teachers who had no part in goal identification. As noted in Chapter Three, terminal goals are statements that generally describe learner capabilities upon completing the school music program. The following group of terminal goals was developed by a school music staff and is not intended as anything other than a proposed list:

> School music should provide each student with the opportunity for aesthetic fulfillment. Upon finishing school music, the student:
> 1. should be able to make reasoned decisions about what he does with music for the rest of his life;
> 2. should exhibit musical tolerance;
> 3. should have a cursory acquaintance with musical symbology and vocabulary;
> 4. should have acquired the tools for a creative and recreative experience;
> 5. should be cognizant of the contribution of music to culture.

Note the obvious lack of clarity that allows for implementation in music classes with varying content and experiences. Another set of goals are those set forth in a tentative statement by Michigan Music Educators:

> 1. Develop musical skills.
> 2. Acquire knowledge and understanding of music from all historical periods, styles, forms, and cultures, and the various functions of music in contemporary, pluralistic society.
> 3. Make rational choices in musical situations, e.g., judge quality of musical performances.
> 4. Respond with feeling to the expressive elements and line of the music.

Some systems use decidedly more specific language to identify terminal goals. Consider the following:

1. Given a specific piece of melodic material, the graduate can recreate the music using voice or instrument with 75 percent accuracy. Accuracy includes correctness in pitch, rhythm, and interpretive cues.

2. Confronted with stimuli in the form of pitch, the graduate can indicate differences and likenesses between pairs of pitches with 80 percent accuracy. Discrepancies between pitches will vary between 10 and 50 cents.

3. Given the stimulus of a four-measure melody, the graduate can, after two auditory impingements, write the melody with 50 percent accuracy. Accuracy includes pitch, intervalic distance, and rhythm.

In almost all communities the foregoing goals would be considered visionary. However, true musical literacy includes behavioral capabilities in each of the categories. The appropriateness of these statements to any other community is, of course, open to question. Nevertheless, the statements do describe something about the graduate as a result of music education.

The development of a similar list of goals is crucial to the curriculum development process in any school district. As indicated in Chapter Three, program and instructional objectives come from goals. Objectives form the foundation upon which instructional content decisions are made.

OBJECTIVES AS THE KEY TO CONTENT

Clearly, a glossary of carefully stated objectives that precisely identifies learning intent will indicate the bulk of instructional content. Decisions on content can be made simultaneously with decisions on objectives. It is possible for the total structure of musical knowledge to be broken down into instructional bits identifiable through objectives. This makes it necessary for music staffs to decide what to teach, selecting the best among the host of possibilities open. The basic content of a music instructional program will be musical in terms of skills, affect, knowledge, and perception. Nonmusical learning outcomes should be secondary in importance.

Music in General Education[3] definitively identified the instructional content of school music as follows:

1. *Elements of music.* Rhythm, melody, harmony, timbre are the elements of music designated by Ernst. Reimer adds form as a basic element.

---

[3] Karl D. Ernst and Charles L. Gary, *Music in General Education* (Washington, D.C.: Music Educators National Conference, 1965), pp. 17–156.

2. *Form or design in music.* Ernst breaks down problems in form as: perceiving unity and contrast, texture, and the development of musical concepts deal with the development of a musical idea.

3. *Interpretive aspects of music.* Study the problems of performance as they deal with dynamics, tempo phrasing, articulation, and media.

4. *Science of sound.* Study basic acoustical facts, the dimensions of tone, and functions of the human ear.

5. *The musical score.* Learn to interpret musical symbols both as a performer and as a non-performer.

6. *Historical considerations.* Study of the music in relation to mankind's past of Western, African, Oriental societies, the treasure house of past music from all cultures.

7. *Music and man.* Explore the relationship between man's need to express himself artistically in relation to social, spiritual, intellectual, and political functions.

8. *Music as a form of expression.* Study the communicative value of music and the way in which it expresses human feeling.

9. *Types of musical performance.* Study all musical performing media in order to gain insight into the multiplicity of expressive possibilities.

10. *Relationship of music to other disciplines in the humanities.* Through humanities, allied arts, and non-performing music classes study the relationship or lack of them among the arts and letters.

11. *Music today.* Study the role of music in contemporary society and in the specific community. Investigate the wide variety of music evident and what purposes each serves.

Aside from the obvious historical, anthropological, and sociological implications of numbers 6, 7, and 10 Ernst's list refers solely to music phenomena. As Murphy[4] states, "Musicianship is the aggregate of individual aptitudes, insights and skills in respect to music. It is based primarily upon two related elements: aesthetic and aural response to tone." Hence, the content of music instruction must stem from the materials of music, its performance, and the record of man and his interaction with music.

CLASSIFYING CONTENT

In order to deal comprehensively with the content/objective problem teachers must develop a means of classifying musical learnings. If music educators lack a clearly defined theory of musical intelligence or an organized description of musical knowledge, they can turn to several gen-

---

[4] Howard Murphy, *Teaching Musicianship* (New York: Coleman Ross Co., Inc., 1950), p. 216.

eralized classification systems of learning outcomes. The most widely used classification system is that developed by Bloom, Krathwohl, and Masia.[5] Two taxonomies have been developed by the writing team: one for cognitive learnings and the other for affective outcomes. A more recent Office of Education study by Elizabeth Simpson has generated a tentative taxonomy of psychomotor or skill objectives.

Unfortunately, all music learning does not conveniently fit into the classification system set forth in the taxonomies. Taxonomies are hierarchical in nature. Many music behaviors are complex and embrace more than one kind of behavior. The evidence of musical behaviors that transcend pure cognitive, affective, or psychomotor operations is overwhelming. In many ways, a classification that allows for interactions of complex musical mental operations may be much more appropriate for the curriculum development team.

Nevertheless, no clear multidimensional classification system is at hand. In order that curriculum builders can look at the problems of identifying objectives and content in music by some means of classification a review of the taxonomies is necessary.

The cognitive domain, emphasizing the mental processes, begins with the concrete behavior of knowledge recall and continues through the more abstract process of analysis, synthesis, and evaluation. The various levels are identified in Table 4.1. An appropriate musical operation is indicated at each level.

Note that each level of the domain identifies a different mental activity on a simple to complex continuum. Nevertheless, when an appropriate musical behavior is identified with each level, it rarely involves *only* a mental operation. Although the hierarchical classification provides a method for thinking about music learning objectives, it does not sharply isolate the components of any given behavior. The need for some multidimensional means of classifying music learning outcomes seems obvious.

Another taxonomy was developed in order to classify values and interests of learners. The affective domain behavior variables are defined as the interest, attitudes, appreciations, and adjustments of the individual. In recent years we have reached a point in the teaching/learning process at which we are concerned not only with the knowledge gained, but also with the willingness of the student to identify himself with a given subject. The affective domain begins with the simple behaviors of receiving

---

[5] Benjamin S. Bloom, ed., *A Taxonomy of Education Objectives. Handbook I: The Cognitive Domain (1956), Handbook II: The Affective Domain (1964)* (New York: David MacKay Co., Inc.).

Table 4.1

Level	Operation or Process	Music Application
Knowledge	Involves the recognition and recall of facts and specifics.	The music learner recalls labels for musical symbols ♩, ♪, ♩, 𝄾 etc.
Comprehension	The learner interprets, translates, summarizes, or paraphrases given material.	The music learner rings appropriate tone bells from non-rhythmic staff notation.
Application	Involves the use of material in a situation different from the one in which it was originally learned.	The music learner sight reads novel patterns of notation.
Analysis	Involves separating a complex whole into its parts until the relationship among the elements is made clear.	The music learner labels unique events in melody, harmony, rhythm, experience.
Synthesis	Involves combining elements to form a new original entity.	Given restricted rhythmic, harmonic, and melodic elements to manipulate, the music learner creates a musical entity.
Evaluation	Involves acts of decision making, judging, or selecting based on a given set of criteria. (These criteria may be objective or subjective.)	Using specific criteria other than emotional inclination, the music learner evaluates a musical composition new to him.

and attending and continues through the complex process of value characterization (see Table 4.2).

Only four levels of the affective domain seem appropriate for consideration here. The highest level deals with a total complex life structure that dictates all behavior patterns of the individual. Significant and continuous involvement in some way with music throughout life does indicate a value dimension of one's outlook. This viewpoint is so deeply enmeshed with an overall life pattern that it is difficult to separate as a pursuable educational objective in the music program.

THE PSYCHOMOTOR DOMAIN

Almost all music educators are disposed to the teaching of musical skills. Traditionally, society has evaluated musical ability solely with performance skill as the criterion. For performing artists, no other criterion is rational. Unfortunately, society has attempted to equate the musically educated with the same criterion, that is, performance skill. This position is, of course, totally unacceptable because motor skills and physiological equipment vary from one individual to another. An individual does not have to be a concert performer in order to be musically educated. At the same time, one cannot be musically educated without substantial music-producing experiences. Music is a form of human experience and behavior; a learner cannot acquire the effects of these experiences vicariously. Since music educators attach great significance to the development of motor skills, a central position in music education curricula must be assigned to performance experiences. Many argue that performing puts the learner closest to the essence of music. There are, however, many levels of performance appropriate to the variety of music classes offered.

In recent years there has been a shift from motor skill achievement for its own sake to motor skill achievement as an avenue to musical understanding. It is crucial that music learners produce and experience music in order to gain in musical understanding. If the teacher is wise, he will see that knowledge of music comes alive during performance. Nebulous, abstract concepts are finally solidified during the music-making experience.

Sequential growth and development of music skills must be carefully planned and teachers should be constant observers and evaluators of student progress. The kinds of behavior that can be classified as psychomotor skills must be categorized within a hierarchical scheme as have cognitive and affective objectives. According to Bloom, "although we recognize the existence of this domain, we find so little done about it in secondary schools and colleges, that we do not believe the development of

Table 4.2

Level	Operation or Process	Music Application
Receiving	The learner is aware of or passively attending to certain phenomena and stimuli, i.e., listening.	The music learner attends to a musical recording being played in the classroom.
Responding	The learner complies to given expectations by attending to or reacting to certain stimuli or phenomena, i.e., interests.	The music learner records answers on an assigned music listening task during a music class (tallies beats, counts theme statements, etc.).
Valuing	The learner displays behavior consistent with a single belief or attitude in situations in which he is not forced to comply or obey, i.e., internal commitment consistent with external behavior.	The music learner spends Sunday afternoon viewing TV program of concert. He can recall events of interest during class discussion on Monday.
Organization	The learner is committed to a set of values as displayed by his behavior, i.e., successful internalization of values.	The music learner practices and constantly seeks musical involvement. More typically, the latter behavior would result in out-of-school confrontations with music.
Characterization	The total behavior of the learner is consistent with the values he has internalized, i.e., philosophy of life—totally behaving as you believe.	No application in music because musical values are only one kind of life value.

a classification of these objectives would be very useful at present."[6] The opinion of the Taxonomy Committee notwithstanding, a research project funded by the United States Office of Education has led to a tentative taxonomy for the psychomotor domain.[7] The scheme is hierarchical in nature and helpful in organizing objectives, subsequent instructional practice, and evaluation procedures.

Simpson's proposed taxonomy of the psychomotor domain has perception at the 1.00 level. Perception is thought to be simple sensory awareness. For music learners this could include feeling, hearing, and seeing some manifestation of sound. For advanced music learners it could mean memorizing and singing a lengthy, intricate melody. The difficulty of only a single level of the domain dealing with perception is quickly seen. Music is an aural art and calls for highly sophisticated aural perceptive abilities. There is a valid argument for a separate hierarchical domain of music perceptive behaviors. This taxonomy might include awareness of (1) sound quality (nonpitched sound patterns, pitched sound patterns); (2) memory for sound (melodic memory, harmonic memory); and (3) formal awareness through memory. The issue at hand is not to propose this taxonomy but to cause readers to be aware of the weakness of the Simpson Taxonomy in providing for multilevel perceptive behavior. Behaviors that are standard, or that should be standard, to the practicing musician are, therefore, valuable in some measure or degree for one who received minimal musical training in school music instruction programs. Almost all so-called music aptitude tests attempt to measure behavior on an easy to difficult continuum of aural perception. Whether or not these skills are innate or learned is an issue for the psychologists. It is known that people can perceive sound more acutely with practice.

The implication is that aural perception ought to be a major concern for the music educator. Appropriate learning sequences and precise identification of aural behaviors at various musical growth levels are necessary. Identification of perceptual objectives along a simple to sophisticated continuum should be a responsibility of the music educator.

Simpson raises the issue, Is there perhaps a sixth major category which might be designated as adapting and originating? One writer has included each of these as a higher level in the domain. For present purposes it seems crucial to include both adaptation and origination as

---

[6] *Ibid.*, pp. 7, 8.

[7] Elizabeth Jane Simpson, *The Classification of Educational Objectives, Psychomotor Domain* (Urbana, Ill.: University of Illinois, 1966), final report U.S. Office of Education Contract No. OE 5–85–104.

Table 4.3

Level	Operation or Process	Music Application
Perception	Sensory awareness.	The music learner distinguishes between music and noise.
Set	Inclined and prepared to initiate motor activity.	The music learner assumes proper playing position for instrument.
Guided Response	Rote activity given perception and inclination.	The music learner imitates clapped-rhythm patterns with duple sub-division of 8 pulse duration.
Mechanism	Skillful habitual response to a motor task.	The music learner performs warmup, scale, and arpeggio patterns without error.
Complex Overt Response	Effortless, quick precise motor response to stimuli.	The music learner sight reads a musical passage with little error.

After Elizabeth Jane Simpson, *The Classification of Educational Objectives, Psychomotor Domain* (Urbana, Ill.: University of Illinois, 1966).

levels 6.0 and 7.0 of the psychomotor domain. Colwell states, "They (adaptation and origination) seem to be valid levels for the development of musical skills but depend upon the creative insight of the performer himself rather than upon the guidance of the teacher."[8] The point is well taken; nevertheless, the opportunity to adapt or originate can be a part of music performance learning experiences arranged by a skilled teacher. A learner does not gain security in adapting without the support of reinforcement from a teacher figure. Learning experiences can, do, and should occur on this level.

Adaptation is defined as the ability to modify existing motor behaviors to accommodate novel situations. Many times conductors demand different motor performance patterns to new situations. Often distinctly new motor skills are needed. The ability to derive an acceptable solution that results in artistic performance without the aid of instruction is a high-level behavior not common in all learners. Simpson cautions against the total acceptance of her taxonomy. She states clearly it is tentative, subject to modification, open for research, and prepared for criticism. Refinement will come from teachers and curriculum makers as they seek to clarify and define objectives appropriate to the psychomotor domain.

OTHER HIERARCHICAL SCHEMES

Another system of classifying learning outcomes in behavioral form is proposed by Woodruff.[9] He allows for interaction between overt or covert responses, decisions, and behaviors of verbal and nonverbal nature. Type I responses are covert, nonverbal, and can be either cognitive or affective in nature. Typical behaviors are observing, perceiving, recognizing, discovering, separating, differentiating, deducing, inferring, selecting, choosing, and comparing. All activity is nonobservable by another teacher and describes a form of mental activity. Type II behaviors are overt, verbal expressions and all products of Type I responses and decisions. Action verbs that imply the appropriate activity include identify, verbally describe or express, repeat, reiterate, classify, codify, and arrange hierarchically. The last category of behaviors are overt nonverbal displays of Type I decisions. Woodruff lists locating, evolving, producing, shaping, making, composing, singing, playing, replicating as appropriate Type III activities.

---

[8] Richard Colwell, *The Evaluation of Music Teaching and Learning* (Englewood Cliffs, N.J.: Prentice-Hall, Inc., 1970).

[9] Asahel Woodruff, *Types of Human Response to Environment,* Mimeographed Paper, 1968.

In a music learning situation a Type I activity could be as follows: Given the aural stimulus of a paired melodic fragment, the student compares for likeness and differences. When the student responds with, "Melody 2 is different from Melody 1," he has exhibited a Type II verbal behavior of an elementary nature. If through bodily motion the student shows an awareness of the difference between the two melodies (e.g., pitch or rhythmic pattern), he is indicating a Type III behavior. In any event, the careful analysis of musical acts into components is helpful in determining the scope of instructional content. The use of learning classification systems for music is important to the curriculum development process. Krathwohl notes:[10]

> In building a curriculum you have undoubtedly paused to consider, "Are there things left out—behaviors I'd have included if I'd thought of them?" The taxonomy, like the period table of elements or a check-off shopping list, provides the panorama of objectives. Comparing the range of the present curriculum with the range of possible outcomes may suggest additional goals that might be included.

Two other advantages are also noted:

1. comparison with others according to the taxonomic framework;
2. aid in the development of sequence.

It is perhaps helpful to suggest tentatively a two-dimensional matrix for classifying human musical behavior (see Figure 4.4). One dimension reflects the materials of music and the other broadly categorizes the mode of response.

WHAT WILL CONTENT BE?

The final decision on what will be taught is a local staff decision. If objectives are clearly stated, content problems should be readily resolved. Nothing should be included because it is traditional. Conversely, all that is innovative is not best. School staffs should be free to draw on the best of old and new extremes and make decisions appropriate for the local system. If music is to be studied, a careful analysis of the structure of

---

10 David R. Krathwohl, "The Taxonomy of Educational Objectives—Its Use in Curriculum Building," in *Contemporary Thought on Public School Curriculum*, E. C. Short and G. D. Marconnit, eds. (Dubuque: William C. Brown, Publishers, 1968), p. 278.

musical knowledge should be made. This information, complete with a definitive plan for when to teach what, can produce a meaningful curriculum.

A TENTATIVE MATRIX FOR MUSIC OBJECTIVES	RHYTHM	MELODY	HARMONY	STRUCTURE	TIMBRE	MUSICAL EXPRESSION	TEXTURE	TOTAL MUSICAL ENTITY
FEELINGFUL OPERATION								
VERBAL OPERATION								
MUSIC OPERATION								
CREATIVE OPERATION								

FIGURE 4.4

Feelingful Operation

A nonverbal inner response, either reflexive or learned, to musical stimuli. Nonmeasurable and most germane to the aesthetic essence of the object of confrontation. Best described as human feeling.

Verbal Operation

An overt manifestation of perceptive, cognitive, or motor response to musical stimuli. Provides a base for measurement of perceptions and various levels of mental operations by manipulating verbal symbols through writing and/or speaking.

Musical Operation

Motor activity that brings about the production of music through singing or playing. Again, an outward manifestation of measurable response to aural or visual musical stimuli.

Creative Operation

Instant or reasoned production of a musical art object in the form of new or renewed performance.

Physical, intellectual, and emotional characteristics of children will help to determine when to teach certain elements of music knowledge. All decisions on what to teach remain for teachers because decisions are a part of the teacher's art.

SUMMARY

The content of instruction in the music education curriculum is based upon the phenomena of music itself. The selection of content is a teacher responsibility once clear-cut statements of objectives are developed. Content should be selected in terms of validity, objectives, student needs, breadth, and learnability. The relationship of classification systems of educational objectives to the problem of content is strong. Systems of classification, such as the Taxonomy of Educational Objectives, provide important means of relating objectives, content, and learning experiences.

ACTIVITIES FOR DISCUSSION AND STUDY

1. Write an objective for a music class for each level of each learning domain.
2. Develop a hierarchical classification system for aural competencies in music.
3. Propose a system for classifying music learning objectives that is more than two-dimensional and allows for interactions between different behavior categories.
4. Choose one of the areas of content identified in Music in General Education and write a sequential group of objectives that might implement the area.
5. Develop a sequence of motor skill abilities for your major instrument.
6. Collect information from neighboring school systems that answers the question, "How did you arrive at instructional content?"

SUPPLEMENTARY READINGS

Ernst, Karl D., and Charles L. Gary, *Music in General Education*. Washington, D.C., Music Educators National Conference, 1965.

Lindvall, C. M., ed., *Defining Educational Objectives.* Pittsburgh: University of Pittsburgh Press, 1964.

Saylor, J. Galen, and William M. Alexander, *Curriculum Planning for Modern Schools.* New York: Holt, Rinehart & Winston, 1966.

Smith, B. O., W. O. Stanley, and J. H. Shores, *Fundamentals of Curriculum Development* (rev. ed.) Yonkers-on-Hudson, N.Y.: World Book Company, 1957.

Taba, Hilda, *Curriculum Development: Theory and Practice.* New York: Harcourt, Brace Jovanovich Inc., 1962.

Trump, J. Lloyd, and Delmas F. Miller, *Secondary School Curriculum Improvement.* Boston: Allyn & Bacon, 1968.

CHAPTER
FIVE

learning experiences and instructional sequence

A significant part of the curriculum development obligation is the identification of learning experiences and their appropriate sequencing. Teachers need to know what kinds of experiences are necessary to achieve a specific set of program objectives and what the logically preferred order might be. This chapter is concerned with aiding in the discovery of what learning path to follow. Instructional efficiency and learning efficiency go hand in hand. Teachers must define the most efficient way to ensure learner success or else as instructional managers they do not fulfill an important commitment. A central teacher role is to develop learning strategies that provide the most effective route of meeting and surpassing objectives for all learners. Naturally, all learners cannot succeed in the same way. There can be, however, an order for the acquisition of musical principles—a simple to complex continuum of learning.

THE NATURE OF MUSIC-LEARNING EXPERIENCES

Where a music educator arranges for students to come in contact with music, learning can take place. A guided interaction between the learner and music is defined as a music-learning experience. The learner must be active during the interaction, for student activity, not teacher activity, brings about learning. However, merely exposing the student to music is unlikely to result in substantial learning gains. The experience ought to have structure, and upon completing the experience, the learner should be aware of his success or lack of it. There also should be purpose and direction to the experience.

There are three significant ways in which a learner can come in contact with music:

1. performing,
2. listening,
3. creating.

Performing is defined as the presence of physiological activity aimed at initiating or responding to music phenomena. As defined, performance could include either refined motor activity related to music notation or rhythmic responses in the form of bodily motion. The first of these two classifications includes singing and instrumental performance and the second embraces all other forms of physical response.

Listening is defined as an auditory interaction. Evidence that there is attention to aural phenomena can only be obtained through either a verbal or a motor behavioral response related to the material being perceived. Although no overt response may be visible, it does not preclude the existence of attention on the part of the listener. If teachers want to be positive that students are attending, some form of overt response is necessary.

The final category of interaction, that of creativity, is difficult to differentiate. It requires a unique kind of mental activity. The outcome is a musical event and could include a wide variety of behaviors. The experience can be improvisatory or of a more deliberate compositional nature. Given limited elements of music a student can at any given age produce a musical entity. Six-year-olds allowed one sound durational value and two pitches could create a ten-second musical happening. This experience provides a unique way of interacting with music. It is distinctly different from either performing or listening. In many ways, a creative exercise of this kind is an inclusive kind of experience in that the act of creation leads to performing and listening events. Several recently proposed musical curricula offer these experiences as the very center of learning.

Writers in the curriculum development field have contributed extensively to knowledge about educational experiences. For example, Tyler lists five general principles for selecting learning experiences:[1]

---

[1] Ralph Tyler, *Basic Principles of Curriculum and Instruction* (Chicago: The University of Chicago Press, 1950).

1. Learning experiences should provide a means of practicing "the kind of behavior implied by the objective."
2. Experiences should provide a basis for obtaining satisfaction from "carrying on the kind of behavior implied by the objective."
3. Experiences should be "appropriate to the student's present attainment, his predisposition and the like."
4. Experiences should be multiple in type with regard to any given objective. "Many particular experiences can be used to attain the same education objectives."
5. Experiences can lead to a variety of outcomes.

Each of Tyler's criteria are well known to almost all teachers. Number 3 is often termed, "begin where the students are," a well-known educational truism. Number 1 suggests that we should teach those things for which we expect to hold pupils accountable. Number 2 refers to reinforcement and the self-assuredness built up through successful experiences. Both numbers 4 and 5 refer to the universe of possibilities available to the teacher and the multiplicity of outcomes possible. The purpose is not to oversimplify Tyler's criteria but to point out that teachers are well informed about the simple but powerful truths of teaching. Implementation, however, is another problem of huge proportion.

Another curriculum writer, Hilda Taba, cautions against confusing content with experiences, as follows:

> It is important to understand that the curriculum consists of two different things: The content and the learning experiences, or the mental operations that students employ in learning content.

Later she states,

> The objectives described as acquisition of knowledge—the concepts, ideas and facts to be learned—can be implemented by the selection of content. On the other hand, the attainment of objectives such as thinking, skills and attitudes cannot be implemented by selection and organization of content alone. To attain them, students need to undergo certain experiences which give them an opportunity to practice the desired behaviors.[2]

If, in fact, music educators want students to perceive music in a mentally active manner with knowledge of its content, analytical listening experiences must be a central feature of the curriculum.

It is clear that decisions on what students will do in order to at-

---

2 Hilda Taba, *Curriculum Development: Theory and Practice* (New York: Harcourt, Brace & World, Inc., 1962).

tain given objectives are crucial ones. Before turning to more precise planning and identification of experiences, it is vital to look at the sequence/learning problem as it effects classroom activity.

SEQUENCE AND LEARNING

As Tyler and others have noted, it is important to identify learning experiences that reflect the learner's level of attainment. Similarly, guided student activity in the classroom ought to reflect the best of what is know about human learning in music. There are several approaches open to the curriculum developer confronted with the problem of sequencing. Probably the most acceptable approach is one that accounts for the nature of the task in relation to the structure of musical knowledge. There is a simple to complex continuum for almost all music outcomes. This continuum is irrevocably tied to the kind of learning necessary for step-by-step achievement.

The nature of music learning is largely a mystery. Little substantial music-learning research is reported in the professional literature. Some methodological studies are extant, but few, if any, precise studies in the step-by-step acquisition of music behaviors are available. An explanation for this dearth may well be the lack of a testable theory of musical intelligence. In any event, the curriculum builder in music education has little to rely on regarding the phenomena of music learning even if he has been able to state his terminal goals and program objectives. Yet, final program development will depend greatly on decisions regarding student learning. It is crucial that some clear pattern of learning sequence be identified that accounts for the complexity of motor, perceptive and verbal music learning.

LEARNING THEORIES

No one learning theory will fit all learning situations in any subject matter area. Learning theorists have not been successful in describing learning theories that account for capability changes of all behavior including both simple and complex dimensions. For instance, the early music learner who distinguishes between two and three meters with verbal accuracy is not functioning the same way as a junior-high student who can identify chord qualities by differences. A high-school singer who can think abstractly where the next pitch will be displays a different but related capability from the sixth-grader who sings two or three intervals by association. It is irrelevant to detail the beliefs about learning held by

Thorndike, Pavlov, Watson, Köhler, and Ebbinghaus. Rather, a position coincident with Gagné will be briefly described. He has specified eight different kinds of learning on a simple to complex continuum. (See Fig. 5.1).[3]

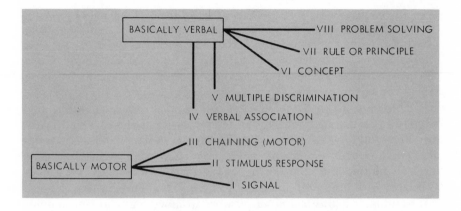

FIGURE 5.1   GAGNÉ HIERARCHY OF LEARNING TYPES

Gagné writes about learning in actuality rather than in theory. The first three or four levels of Gagné's learning hierarchy relate to motor learning only. Motor learning, the control of physiological processes, has long enjoyed a place of centrality among early music educational experiences. The different levels of learning are most identifiable by conditions within the learner himself and the learning situation. Gagné has adopted this viewpoint because of the obvious need to have an explanation for many kinds of human capability change. In reality, Thorndike, Skinner, and Hull are among several psychologists who perceived the necessity for outlining kinds of multiple learning. The present task is not to be bogged down in theoretical discussion, but to describe learning conditions for eight varieties of learning situations. In each case there will be one or two examples of music learning that illustrate the kind in question. The significance of carefully describing the various kinds of learning is the need for care in projecting, arranging, and carrying out instructional strategies. The level of learning is defined by a program of instructional objectives. Subsidiary learning experiences of either motor or verbal nature can be identified that will culminate in the higher-level concept, rule, or problem-solving capability.

---

[3] Robert Gagné, *The Conditions of Learning* (New York: Holt, Rinehart & Winston, Inc., 1965).

I Signal Learning

"The individual learns to make a general diffuse response to a signal. This is the classical conditioned response of Pavlov (1927)."[4]

There are probably very few teacher-led instances of signal learning peculiar to music education, but one example is the attention-getting signal of rapping the conductor's stand. The period of quiet (if any) that follows this teacher behavior can be attributed to signal learning. There is a generalized response to the signal of baton hitting—usually based on fear of consequence.

Similarly, there is reason to believe that early, infantile free responses (usually rhythmic) to music are also examples of signal learning. The sound in this case provides the signal to some kind of gross undifferentiated body movement that is very often crudely rhythmic. The form of the response need not be refined in any sense and is very often associated with pure pleasure and joy of perceiving and reacting to musical stimulus. It is this feeling of pleasure in movement and concomitant gratification that provide the necessary motivation for learning to take place.

S		R
Musical		Motor
sound	$\longrightarrow$	response
		(pleasure)

According to Gagné,[5] "In order for signal learning to occur, there must be a natural reflex, typically a reflexive emotional response (startle, fear, anger, *pleasure*), on the part of the learner." In the instance of music learning cited, a kind of kinesthetically rewarding experiences is evident. It is conceivable that this kind of free gross response might be new to a few kindergartners, nursery schoolers, and Head Start participants. Here learning would be almost instantaneous. The child who has not experienced would learn by observing his peers.

Successful signal learning is best achieved when the teacher remembers two important characteristics: (1) The stimulus events produce the desired response when the timing between their occurrence is minimal. Learning psychologists refer to the interval of time as contiguity. Events must happen quickly—almost simultaneously. (2) There is strong evidence to support the claim that the more times learners are exposed to the

---

[4] *Ibid.*, p. 58.

[5] *Ibid.*, p. 65.

signal-learning sequence, the quicker and stronger the learning. This simply means that repetition is a must for efficient learning to take place. Signal learning is basic to all other learning in music in that it provides a framework of *awareness* to musical sound.

II STIMULUS-RESPONSE LEARNING

"The learner acquires a precise response to a discriminated stimulus." $(S_s \rightarrow R)$[6]

Music-learning experiences in the early elementary years are full of examples of stimulus-response learning. An example might be a child's ability to match a pitch given by the teacher with his own voice.

Stimulus-response learning is seen as a gradual process in which the learner discriminates the correct response. The matching of pitch is a particularly good example because of the lack of any prerequisite verbal knowledge. In learning pitch matching the student must perceive the stimulus (a sound from some source) and make a carefully differentiated response. The muscle set of the vocal chords helps to determine whether or not the pitch heard will be the pitch sung. To get the right feeling or kinesthesis of the muscles requires cultivation and repetition. Hence, both perception of the stimulus and internal muscle set are necessary for the desired response to be initiated. It is this inner set that makes stimulus-response learning different from signal learning.

$$\text{Piano or} \longrightarrow S_s \longrightarrow R$$
teacher
pitch

Muscular set of   Sung pitch
pitch-producing
mechanism

The response, in the form of matched pitch, is usually subject to favorable comment by the teacher. Very often this praise is sufficient to reinforce the response and bring about learning. The words "well done" or "that's right" provide the very necessary reinforcement and attendant learner's feeling of satisfaction. Similarly, the child can cue from non-verbal signs emitted by the teacher. In any case, there is a terminal motor act that provides an observable behavior for evaluation.

Three factors contribute to the success of stimulus-response learning: (1) reinforcement, (2) time between response and reinforcement, and

---

[6] *Ibid.*, p. 58.

(3) multiple presentation of stimulus (repetition). In reinforcement the elicited behavior must result in satisfaction to the learner. As noted, school learning behavior of this kind is usually reinforced with praise, or better yet with self-awareness of success. The time lapse between performance and reinforcement should be short. In the case of pitch matching each correct response should be immediately reinforced. In the future of music education computer-assisted instruction may provide instantaneous reinforcement of a pitch-matching response. Repetition is extremely important in music learning, particularly when it relates to aural perception. Drill is unavoidable. There is no magic method to circumvent the need for drill. In the example, pitch matching is achieved first at a frequency comfortable to the learner (e.g., c_1). He must also learn to use other areas of his voice. The precise muscle sets for each pitch calls for minute kinesthetic discriminations. This refined motor behavior is only developed after carefully controlled practice involving adequate reinforcement for all pitch-producing behaviors. Obviously, five- and six-year-old learners are more likely to achieve an accurate, gross body response to a specific meter rather than match a pitch by singing an open vowel.

III Chaining

Chaining is evident when learners can perform a motor act involving a sequence of individual S_s-R. Gagné identifies starting an automobile, turning on a television set, reciting a poem as examples of chaining. In music learning, producing certain pitches on an instrument or singing a song from memory are examples of this level of learning. Clearly, this kind of behavioral change involves both verbal and nonverbal activities. Since these acts are different in substance, motor learning will be referred to as *chaining* and verbal as *verbal association*.

In order to have an example of chaining, assume a situation in which the learner is to respond to three note placements on a one-line staff.

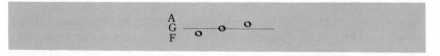

The one line is identified as G. The player is to play pitches F, G, and A on the tone bells when he perceives the note on the staff. After a few trials he is able to do this with complete accuracy. For each response, the chain could be diagrammed as follows:

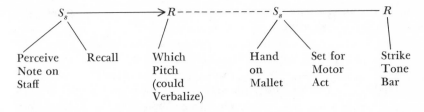

Perceive	Recall	Which	Hand	Set for	Strike
Note on		Pitch	on	Motor	Tone
Staff		(could	Mallet	Act	Bar
		Verbalize)			

In this chain two *S-R*'s are needed before the chain can be learned. The learner must be able to (1) perceive and identify the note placement on the staff and (2) grasp mallet correctly and strike the correct key. Other motor chains often have many more S_s-*R*'s.

The acquisition of chains can be facilitated by verbal instructions to the learner, but the most efficient learning can be accomplished with minimal verbal instructions. In the instance above, giving names to the notes (F, G, A) may create more efficient learning. Verbal instructions or the manipulation of the learning situation are designed to eliminate errors and mistrials, i.e., ensure precision and correctness in the individual S_s-*R*. Occasionally, the learner provides his own verbal cues. For example, in the above hypothetical situation, the learner might well refer to different notes as "one above," or "one below" the pitch G. When the learner can finally perform the chain, he no longer needs his nor anyone's verbal cues either in relation to the individual S_s-*R*'s or the chain itself. In order to establish behavioral chains for learners, a number of factors are important to the teacher. According to Gagné, "the learner must reinstate" the several S_l-*R*'s in the correct order."[7] Two well-known approaches are possible for those responsible for learning. A teacher can arrange to start from the end of the chain and work backward—something like whole to parts identifying each link. The other approach is to work from beginning to end with many verbal cues and "prompts." In either case, the individual links must be known. The teacher and learner are only concerned with sequencing or precise arrangement of the several S_s-*R*'s.

The time lapse between the events of learning a chain is an important consideration. Individual S_s-*R*'s must be produced in rapid, proper sequence if the chain is to be established efficiently. In the example of playing pitches from a single line score, sound production must follow perception of the note. The motor act of realizing a pitch must follow closely or the overall skill may never be achieved. The proximity of reinforcement is also crucial for efficient learning. Eventually, conscious identification of the pitch name may be totally unnecessary. Reading

---

[7] *Ibid.*, p. 93.

music by distances between notes is probably vastly more efficient and the tactile behavior is a most desirable chain to establish.

Ordinarily, if all conditions are perfect, a chain can be learned on the first trial. In practice, this may not be so because of the individual differences of learners—particularly in how they can handle prompts and cues. Highly exact motor skills demand even more repetition before they can be a part of the learners' behavior. In order to achieve efficient, positive, and precise learning, repetition is necessary. Nevertheless, care must be taken to ensure that only correct S_s-R's in accurate sequence are produced. As in the case of the young pianist, it is quite possible to practice errors to perfection.

In all learning, success in achieving the terminal act should be pleasure-giving to the learner. The learner needs to find satisfaction that provides the reinforcement for that which is done correctly. Gagné states that without reinforcement, the last S_s-R becomes "extinct" and the "chain as a whole disappears."[8]

Among the other variables in learning (extinction, generalization, discrimination, and forgetting) the situation for chaining is much the same as stimulus-response. As noted above, a chain can become extinct when reinforcement is withheld. Generalization is also possible. In the music learning example cited learners could readily move to a differently positioned one-line staff and/or change the location of the hand at the keyboard. In either case, generalization of the particular S_s-R brings about generalization in the chain. Discrimination could be evident if the learner was presented with a two-line staff and was asked to think of G as small g. Here the learner has to readjust completely because of a major difference in the triggering stimulus but he could discriminate quickly and produce the correct response. *Forgetting* a motor chain is an unusual phenomenon. Chains resist loss but the forgetting of one of the links can create a recall problem. Of more importance is the relative speed with which one usually regains a chain once all links are reinstated.

IV VERBAL ASSOCIATION

"Verbal association is the learning of chains that are verbal."[9]

The language communication behaviors found in human beings are unique and provide a special kind of learning phenomenon. Verbal association learning is the ability to name objects or recall longer chains of words as in a memorized poem. On a simple level, if a very young

---

[8] *Ibid.*, p. 94.
[9] *Ibid.*, p. 58.

child were shown a drum and told it was a drum, chances are he would call it by name the next time he saw it. He need not differentiate among a number of drums nor deal with the concept of drums as a class of percussion instruments. He can only name the object at hand a drum. Obviously, this simple behavior is basic to any further learning about drums or percussion and learning communication.

The above example is a verbal chain made up of two S_s-R links. In the first link the learner is presented the object in question. His response is perceptual, i.e., he sees the object. In the second link he is stimulated by the word drum, which he repeats as accurately as possible. Reinforcement should be provided by the person responsible for the learning situation.

Verbal chains may be made up of many more than two links. The instant an individual utters more than one word, he reflects a chain or more than two links. If a learner can recite a formula, recall the words to a song, or recite a memorized poem, he is performing multilink chains of verbal learning. Rote teaching of a song in the early elementary grades is made up of both motor and verbal chaining as such; it is a very complicated learning task. Almost all rote teaching of elementary songs involves a whole-parts-whole approach. Research in verbal associate learning tends to support this method so far as learning words is concerned. However, coupled with added problems of learning a pitch sequence simultaneously, the most efficient way may be different. At any rate, the learner is confronted with the whole and subsequently learns the verbal material in parts, perhaps a phrase at a time. Gagné discusses the use of coding cues to facilitate links between various parts of the chain. The tune may very well serve this purpose for a child learning a song by rote. A wise teacher would take advantage of any peculiarity in the melody. After the child learns the first phrase, he goes on to the second but reiterates the first in moving along. Thus, the learner has the advantage of practicing the first chain as he moves on to the next. Of course, this process is continued until the total chain is developed. Research indicates (Krueger)[10] that the number of links in a chain causes little difference in the number of trials necessary to reach at least 90% learning. Chains of 5, 15, 50, and 100 items were included in this study. The implication is that nine or ten trials will be necessary before learning reaches a level satisfactory to the teacher. There seems to be no way to avoid drill.

In order to provide a situation conducive to learning verbal chains, a number of factors need careful consideration. For a learner to acquire

---

[10] W. C. F. Krueger, "Rate of Progress as Related to Difficulty of Assignment," *Journal of Educational Psychology*, XXXVII, 4 (1946), 247.

a chain, each link must be previously learned as S_s-R. In the example of learning the words to a rote song the learner will have to be able to utter each word. The connections between S_s-R's are vital to learning the chain and are best learned by supplying the learner with connections he already knows. As noted above, the melody of the song being learned may very well assist the learning of some verbal chain. Unfortunately, children pay greater heed to the words than to the tune. Melodic perception functions only as a helping hand to learning the verbal chain.

If a verbal chain is to be taught, the units must be presented in the proper sequence. As noted, the most efficient way seems to be by presenting the chain piece by piece with constant built-in practice over previous segments. Naturally, the chain cannot be learned if the student doesn't make the proper response each time a learning trial takes place. The subtle (kinesthetic) small muscle patterns become automatic and a part of the chain triggering the next link. In the rote song example the student is involved and produces words and tune as he goes along. Both melodic pitch and the activity of word utterance then become an important aid in forging the final, total chain. There seems to be no limitation to the length of chain that can be learned. For immediate recall, chains of seven events (plus or minus two) seem optimal. This kind of memory ability is one that varies from one individual to another. Given the correct learning conditions and the subsequent appropriate response by learners, reinforcement by the teacher must occur. Incorrect or mispronounced words or missed pitches should be dealt with immediately because faulty behaviors can become a part of the chain very quickly. Since in some early elementary music texts word and pitch chains are tedious, reinforcement must come from the teacher because learners are unable to determine the correctness of their responses. An important objective for all aspects of the music education program should be the development of critical evaluation skills for most learners.

Verbal chaining is particularly vulnerable to interference. As the links of long chains are formed, each new connection makes those to come harder to learn and those already learned harder to recall. The most efficient way to overcome this problem is to use a great deal of repetition in the learning situation. Even experienced teachers have been fooled many times when chains are seemingly established. More drill is often needed. Once verbal chains are *firmly* and accurately established, they resist forgetting. If forgetting occurs, it is caused by the breakdown of one or more links of the chain, and it is often the result of interference. Interference is likely to be brought about by learning a similar, but more difficult chain. Extra verses of songs may very well bring about a forgotten first or second verse if the verbal material is similar and slightly more difficult.

V Multiple Discrimination

"The individual learns to make a different identifying response to as many different stimuli, which may resemble each other in physical appearance to a greater or lesser degree."[11] The learner is presented with the problem of learning a number of chains simultaneously, e.g., learning to make the proper playing response to a number of pitches on the treble staff. Suppose that the student is to learn the material in Figure 5.2. Each is a motor chain culminating an overt motor act.

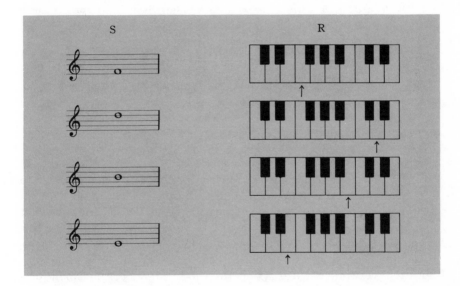

FIGURE 5.2   LEARNING SET FOR BEGINNING PIANIST

Clearly the task is to discriminate among the several stimuli and produce the correct response. In many ways the task is an overwhelming one for the young pianist, and it takes a long time until he can operate with *any* of the stimuli accurately. Ideally, each chain is learned individually and in isolation. But more is needed. Under conditions of performance the learner will have to respond to the stimuli of notation and make the appropriate discrimination while incurring the interference of other chains. The learning task is one of discrimination.

For effective multiple discrimination learning to take place, a number of factors must be carefully controlled.

---

11 Gagné, *op. cit.,* p. 58.

1. The learner must be able to respond correctly to each member of the learning set. The chain for seeing F on the staff and depressing the correct piano key is a prerequisite to discriminating among F, D, B, and E (see Figure 5.2). Similarly, the chain for each of the other pitches needs firm establishment.

2. Because of the nature of the learning task, there is great probability of interference. Interference is caused by the similarity of stimulus and response. This interference calls for repetition in the learning task. Music teachers are quite familiar with the case for drill. Nevertheless, the nature and sequence of the most beneficial drill are not so well known. Some learning theorists consider the latter problem unimportant.

3. As in all S_s-R learning the need for reinforcement is present. Somehow the learner should be able to secure an evaluation of his response immediately. In music much learning takes place individually and without the aid of a teacher. Reinforcement of correct responses in the home practice situation is nonexistent. There is current evidence that children can make comparative judgments if given the proper tools. The ability to evaluate one's responses should grow hand in hand with new responses as they are acquired.

VI CONCEPT LEARNING

"The learner acquires a capability of making a common response to a class of stimuli that may differ from each other widely in physical appearance. He is able to make a response that identifies an entire class of objects or events."[12] Concepts are the building blocks of thought processes. They can have concrete referents and, when acquired, are operational for the learner—he can *use* them in actual stimulus situations. For example, assume that it is important to be knowledgeable about harmony. A learner must know not only the building blocks of harmony but also the flow and connection of these building blocks as well. A concept of triads would be one way in which a person can think abstractly about harmony. It would be useful to him when he is confronted with a listening problem calling for focus on the harmonic elements of the stimulus. He will need more than merely the ability to state "a triad is a chord of three pitches built in thirds." It is unlikely that pure verbalization can help him solve a listening/learning problem. A learner, having acquired an experience-based concept of what triadic harmony is and does, can think abstractly about harmonic events that occur while he listens to a music composition from the eighteenth century.

---

12 *Ibid.*, p. 58.

Similarly, consider the following as an example of conceptual thought:

1. Think of the pitch F-sharp;
2. Think up a perfect fifth;
3. Think down a major second;
4. Think up a minor second;
5. Think up a perfect fourth;
6. Think down a perfect fifth;
7. Think down a perfect fourth.

Thinking through this series of intervals is possible for those who can function abstractly with intervals—a conceptual operation.

How does he learn a concept? What are the prerequisite abilities? Figure 5.3 shows a tentative schemata for learning to deal with triads as a class of aural phenomena. Note that it is necessary for a host of behavioral capabilities to exist before a student reaches the concept-learning level. At the sixth level the learner should be able to differentiate among many harmonic happenings and be precise in identifying the function of triads. It is, of course, simple to establish by rote a glib verbal chain describing triads and their function.

The concept of a triad as an aid to thinking about music is not easily established; much drill and careful reinforcements are vital to the learning sequence. Successfully achieving an objective that involves triads and their use to learners is a tedious, complex process. One who is attempting to produce a triad capability in learners must plan and carry out learning sequences carefully. Each prerequisite behavior must be achieved and well practiced. Learning aural abilities requires aural involvement, for it is impossible to acquire precise aural perception through the teacher's verbalizations. It is impossible to describe how something sounds if it has not actually been heard. Additionally, the wise teacher pursues a multisensory approach. Constant reiteration of the triad concept in use may be made by tactile, visual, and aural stimulation. Correct learner responses are immediately reinforced. Once the learner is able to perceive triads in an harmonic flow and analyze their function, the concept is established. He can answer questions similar to "Where is the triad in the following sound combinations?"

The ability to use concepts in mental operations frees the individual from the specific instances common to *S-R* and chaining learning. In the above example the learner can use his triad concept ability in dealing with any kind of music. He may be listening, viewing, or playing. If the concept of triad is known, it is triggered by many stimulus situations. If

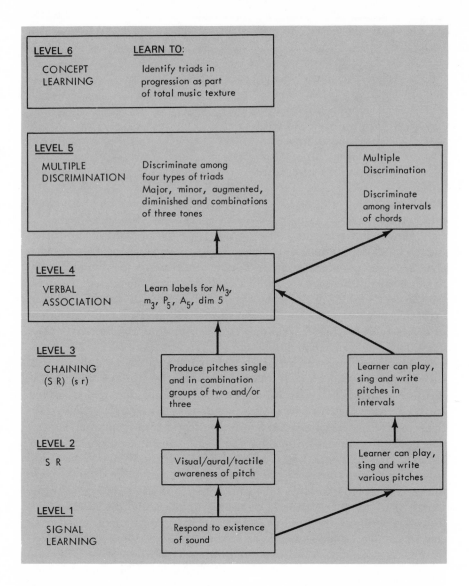

FIGURE 5.3 TENTATIVE LEARNING SCHEMATA
FOR TRIAD FUNCTION IN HARMONY

triad was learned as a single event in a single piece of music (chaining), the learner can only respond to it under similar conditions. Musical behavior thus acquired serves no worthwhile goal. As managers of learning, music educators must develop learning sequences that bring about functional intellectual behaviors.

VII RULE OR PRINCIPLE LEARNING

"A principle is a chain of two or more concepts."[13] As groups and clusters, principles make up the organization of knowledge of a discipline or parts of a discipline. Gagné cites the following as examples of principles: "The sun sets in the west; birds fly south in the winter; or $E = mc^2$."[14] The first example has three concepts, the second four, and the last at least five. A more appropriate example for our purposes might be, "Melodies consist of repeated tones, steps, or leaps." In order to deal with this, a learner must know melody, steps, leaps, and repeated tones as concepts. Technically, he will also have to know the concepts represented by the word "consist." Each concept is made up of a series of lower level learnings including type II through type V. The concepts form a chain that is then designated either a principle of or a rule on the makeup of melodies. Nothing more can be added about melodic rules or principles. If the learner acquires the necessary abilities, he can be said to behave melodically.

As in concept learning, students can quickly parrot the verbal chain, "Melodies consist of repeated tones, steps, or leaps." Teachers often ask for a verbal definition as a terminal ability. It is much more definitive to describe what the learner should be able to do with the rule. Rote verbalization of this principle of melody needs neither ability in writing nor analyzing by ear or eye. Unfortunately, many rules and principles of music are only superficially learned in the typical performance or nonperformance class. Often there is little effort beyond motor/verbal manipulation evident in the average school music class. The several concepts must all be clearly established or else the chain leading to a principle is likely to break down. Learning a principle in this situation is mere verbalization without meaning.

Many principles can be learned by pure verbalization. Adults who have a substantial vocabulary may easily learn a principle from the printed or spoken word. For example, if one knows the concept represented by the word "romantic," he can readily acquire the principle represented by the statement, "Beethoven, Schubert, Schumann, and Mendelssohn are composers of the Romantic period."

---

13 *Ibid.*, p. 58.
14 *Ibid.*, p. 141.

Gagné identifies the following sequence necessary for learning a principle.[15]

"Step 1. Inform the learner about the form of the performance to be expected when learning is completed.

Step 2. Question the learner in a way that requires the reinstatement (recall) of the previously learned concepts that make up the principle.

Step 3. Use verbal statements (cues) that will lead the learner to put the principle together, as a chain of concepts, in the proper order.

Step 4. By means of a question, ask the learner to "demonstrate" one or more concrete instances of the principle.

Step 5. (Optional, but useful for later instruction.) By a suitable question, require the learner to make a verbal statement of the rule."

In accordance with these steps in instruction, consider the following presentation of the rules of melodic motion.

Step 1. *Objective:* Given examples of short musical compositions, by aural or visual stimulation, the learner will be able to differentiate among their melodic texture by classification as:
1. step, leap, step;
2. step, repeat, leap;
3. leap, step;
4. repeated tone, step;
5. leap, step, repeated tone.

Step 2. *Review:* Through verbal statements and questions establish, for certain, the existence of the various concepts. Ask students to write examples of each kind of melodic motion. Learners could also sing or play and then discuss various kinds of melodic motion.

Step 3. After experiencing each kind of melodic motion learners can be cued to the realization of the principle to be learned. There may be statements like: "How else can the melody move?" "This melody involves three kinds of movement." The inspection of student-composed melodies with appropriate verbalization may take place. In music learning as opposed to verbal learning, many aurally perceived examples would be appropriate and necessary. The cues of most value would come from actual music examples, not from specifically composed excerpts.

Step 4. At this point the teacher might ask students for an example of melody that includes all three concepts of motion. In addition, the learner may be asked to differentiate between each kind of motion while he is watching a score and listening to a recorded example. He may also be asked to circle each kind of melodic motion as it occurs.

Step 5. Finally, the learner could be asked to summarize and generalize as follows: Form a general statement that describes how musical melodies move.

---

15 *Ibid.,* p. 149.

The above sequence is only a hypothetical model. Many different kinds of learning activities could be employed. The teacher is, of course, free to manipulate the conditions and the experiences designed to produce the described behaviors. In fact, the value of the skill might be questioned for all learners. As noted, rules or principles form the basis of knowledge of music. The actual performance of music or motor activity could be a level III activity. It is presumed by music education scholars that knowledge of music produces higher-level performance behaviors and, although unproven, the position is probably accurate. An examination of the music practices of the Western world reveals a generalized body of principles about music, which is known as the *organized knowledge* of music. Specifically, Gagné calls the set of principles "the structure of organized knowledge about a topic."[16] This structure is arranged hierarchically in Figure 5.4. Here the topic is harmony in music. Aestheticians believe the acquisition of rules and concepts makes possible a deeper aesthetic experience for the learner.

The structure of knowledge depicted in Figure 5.4 is labeled "Harmonic structure and motion in music." Concepts are indicated on level II. Once the learner reaches level III and, in some cases, level II, he functions on the rule level. Level I is interval perception, a multiple discrimination behavior. The learner is dealing with a class of phenomena definable as distances between pitches. In level II he puts intervals together in sets of more than one and learns the concept of chords and root movement. Level III involves chains of two or more concepts to form principles of harmonic systems and kinds of connections. Higher-order principles constitute level IV in which a learner can identify most, if not all, chords and analyze chord to chord flow. As a whole, the overall principle calls for a behavior that can identify the role of harmony in a musical composition.

According to researchers in verbal learning, each level of the hierarchy is important to successful achievement of the next. There are prerequisites, and learning of substantial proportions depends on their sequential success and presentation. Of course, one must know the necessary order of learning before he begins to teach. Unfortunately, little research is available in music learning that is addressed to learning sequence and order of presentation. According to Ausubel, "organized sets of learning have great resistance to forgetting."[17]

---

16 *Ibid.*, p. 151.

17 David Ausubel, *The Psychology of Meaningful Verbal Learning* (New York: Grune & Stratton, Inc., 1963).

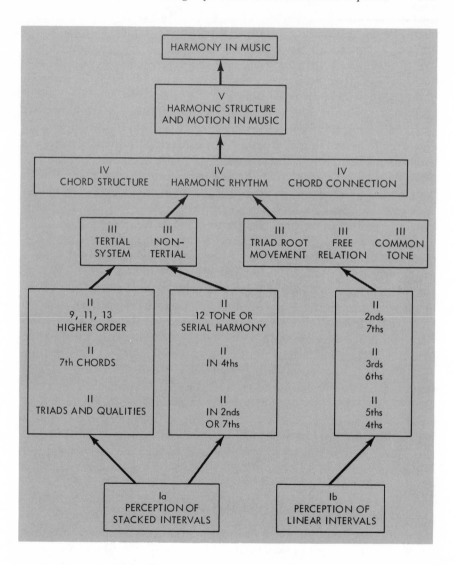

FIGURE 5.4   HARMONY IN MUSIC

VIII PROBLEM SOLVING

"Problem solving is a kind of learning that requires the internal events called thinking. Two or more previously acquired rules or principles are somehow combined to produce a new capability that can be shown to depend on a higher-order principle."[18]

Problem solving is a learning activity in which an individual uses previously learned principles to solve a problem. The successful solution of the problem provides the learner with a new higher-order principle that did not previously exist in his mind. Although the successful solution of the problem might be the objective, the learner also acquires new learning.

Perhaps the following hypothetical situation will serve to clarify problem solving as a kind of learning in music. Suppose students in a musicianship class were presented a problem in form. For the first time they are asked to determine the form of a piece that has five main but repeated thematic elements. Previous experience with form has included only three-part structure. Learners are well acquainted with the principles of contrast, repetition, and overall unity found in three-part forms. Cadence, modulation, phrases, and periods are also a part of the students' perceptual signals. Learners could be exposed to a relatively simple Kodály Second Rondo or a more complex Mendelssohn *Song Without Words*. The music example used should be related to their age and experience. Upon hearing the selection or performing it, learners are led to a formal analysis through careful questioning by the instructor. It is important that he not give the solution away by stating what the example is. Instead, he creates a kind of "discovery" learning situation by guiding the learner in thinking through the problem. Questions asked could include:

1. What keys are used by the composer?
2. How many repetitions of the original theme are there?
3. Sing theme(s) that are in contrast to the first theme.

The learner is led to recalling appropriate principles of musical form. As the experience progresses, he should be able to identify the existence of five distinct sections in the composition. This discovery is made on the basis of known principles and perceptions. He will have acquired the higher-order principle of extended five-part form. As the experience progresses, he should be able to identify the existence of five distinct sections in the composition. This discovery is made on the basis of known principles and perceptions. He will have acquired the higher-order principle of extended five-part form. The instructor will likely have to supply the label for the form (i.e., Second Rondo or five-part song form).

---

18 Gagné, *op. cit.*, p. 58.

Labeling is not of significant importance. The new principles of multiple contrast and repetition leading to expansion are important. Presumably, when learners are again presented with a five-part form, they will make the appropriate behavior of identification and differentiation. Problem solving is a form of discovery learning based upon a solid foundation of previous experiences and a substantial set of principles. If prerequisite experiences are not a part of the learner's behaviors, there is little, if any, hope of problem solving taking place.

THE CONTINUUM OF LEARNING VARIETIES

Each of the foregoing eight kinds of learning lead to different kinds of behavioral change in individuals. Changes in music capability, regardless of level, can be the result of educational experiences. The teacher is accountable for both deciding what experiences are necessary and identifying the nature of learning taking place. Knowledge of the kind of learning involved simplifies and clarifies the process of selecting learning experiences.

SEQUENCING MUSIC LEARNING

Keeping the foregoing in mind, it is possible to make a significant case for a simple to complex continuum of music learning. Any problem solving task involves recall of rules or principles that in turn bring to mind concepts and all the lower-level varieties of learning prerequisite to concept learning.

As a learner progresses to each principle, he must acquire expanding abilities, knowledge, and attitudes toward music learning. This development is a long-term proposition and requires careful sequencing. The identification of appropriate learning structures to serve specific program objectives and the organization of learning experiences sequentially within each structure represent the implementation phase of curriculum development or program planning. The current situation in music education in schools so far as program development is concerned is not good. There is little evidence of deliberate program planning. Some school music staffs have found it impossible even to communicate across vocal/instrumental lines or levels of instruction. Regardless, one should very carefully note Bruner's hypothesis "that any subject can be taught effectively in some intellectually honest form to any child at any stage of development."[19]

---

[19] Jerome Bruner, *The Process of Education* (Cambridge: Harvard University Press, 1961).

BUILDING LEARNING STRUCTURES IN MUSIC

Curriculum planners in music must start by identifying terminal goals and program objectives appropriate to their instructional environment. Necessary learning experiences are clustered into courses that seem logical to meet expected outcomes. Program objectives need definition and the music principles necessary to meet them should be identified and stated. As each music principle is selected, a learning structure can be charted. Figure 5.5 is an example of learning structure, the terminal goal of which deals with rhythmic reading (no pitch). The learning level reached is that of problem solving, type VIII according to Gagné's hierarchy. Students will be able to read in duple and triple simple meter using half, quarter, eighth notes, and rests of equal values. This structure may be learned by children eight, nine, or ten years of age. Naturally, the inclusion of this capability in music education is optional by local music educators. Objectives reflect the value of music in a local educational program and its importance as seen by the community. More specifically, the objective for this structure can be stated:

> Given a notated nonpitched, two-measure musical excerpt in duple or triple meter, learners can tap the pattern with no more than one error at ♩ = 72. Note and rest values used will be ♩ ♩ ♪ 𝄾 𝄾. Errors will include mistakes in duration only. The error unit will be one pulse.

The above objective and the learning structure in Figure 5.5 are only models. There is no universality claimed or intended for this objective. In practice, many alterations in both the objective and structure are possible and potentially desirable, but for this discussion, however, the example is adequate. Many music educators could rethink the process as indicated and come up with some new instructional design. The crucial point is development of a simple to complex learning route in order to establish some specific behavior in music. As the learner progresses to successful completion of the structure, he moves through a logical sequence of learning experiences. Each level is prerequisite to the next. There is no short-cut or glib verbalization over any important phase.

The rhythmic reading learning structure in Figure 5.5 contains both cognitive and psychomotor learning varieties. Also implied is an attitudinal factor that tends to equip the learner with or without necessary motivation. This is not a concern at this time since allowance for motivation is primarily a teacher function and highly individualized within any

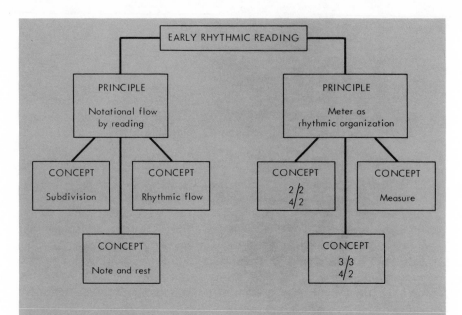

<table>
<tr><td>

Multiple Discriminations

1. Distinguish between 𝅗𝅥 𝅘𝅥 or 𝅘𝅥𝅮 printed.
2. Describe values of each.
3. Identify likenesses and differences between pair patterns.

Verbal Associates

1. State verbal labels for different note values.
2. State verbal labels for rest values.

Chains

1. Tap patterns from memory.
2. Write representations of sound.

S_s _____ R connections

1. Say word rhythms from rote.
2. Tap on cue.
3. Keep time.

</td><td>

Multiple Discriminations

1. Distinguish between 2/4 3/4 from sound.
2. Verbally describe each from aural stimulus.

Verbal Associates

1. State meter definition.
2. Name meters on cue.
3. Measure and define barlines.

Chains

1. Tap stress and nonstress.

S_s _____ R connections

1. Show awareness of twos or threes by body motion.

</td></tr>
</table>

FIGURE 5.5   EARLY RHYTHMIC READING

learning experience. The structure is a hierarchical model utilizing a growing sophistication of learning types. One can assume signal learning as any entry behavior (e.g., learner can perceive sound as music). On either side of the structure the individual learner has to know that he was conscious of musical sound. This awareness is necessary before any of the S_s-R could be established. On the S_s-R level the ability to say word rhythms from rote memory or tap rhythms on visual cue (not musical notation) is desirable. Showing consciousness of metric organization is also crucial. This awareness can be assessed by observing body or arm motion indicative of two- and three-pulse meters. Learners should also be able to keep time with music in two or three meters.

Several motor chains must be established and are prerequisite to any higher-order abilities: (1) Learners must tap patterns from memory after receiving an aural stimulus. If a count or "tah-tee" (Kodály) system is used, it could be introduced at this point in a rote fashion. (2) Another chain is the ability to record the total number of sounds in a rhythm pattern in such a short-hand pattern as ‖ ‖ ‖ ‖ ‖ ‖ ‖ ‖.   (3) Within the meter principle, a learner should be developing an ability to tap or clap stressed or nonstressed sound. Accent awareness is thought to be a necessary prerequisite for meter understanding.

In order to communicate the experience verbally, verbal labels for the musical characters in this learning structure must be acquired. The following vocabulary is appropriate and indispensable:

half note. . . . ♩ (half)	half rest. . . . ▬
quarter note. . ♩	quarter rest. . . 𝄽
eighth note. . . ♪	eighth rest. . . . 𝄾

Definitions of meter, measure, barline, and meter signature numerals are also important.

This is purely verbal learning. The task is to recall a verbal utterance in relation to a symbol or set of symbols visually presented. Verbal ability of this nature may have little to do with the ability to perform patterns correctly, but there is no substitute for the communication value of these verbal labels. Precise labels are appropriate from the beginning of music instruction.

A number of behaviors are important at the multiple discrimination level. Visual and aural discrimination of musical rhythmic sounds and music symbols are invaluable. The ability to differentiate among verbal labels is a prerequisite to the concept level. The following are also believed necessary at the multiple discrimination level:

1. Discriminate among aurally and visually presented non-pitched rhythmic sounds.
2. Verbally describe durational time periods.
3. Differentiate (same/different) among pairs of rhythm patterns.
4. Differentiate rhythms according to their meter (two or three).
5. Verbally describe meter signature figures.

Many more discriminations and drills are likely and possible, for music learning requires drill and drill is particularly helpful in multiple discrimination when preparations are made for concept learning.

At least six concepts are prerequisite to the two principles noted in the learning structure. Concepts of subdivision, note and rest values, rhythmic flow, two meter, and measure are important. The two principles, notational flow and meter organization, are necessary for accurate rhythmic reading, which is a problem-solving activity and functions as a learning experience. While a learner reads and performs each of several patterns, he is increasing his reading power. When confronted with new reading problems, he is more skilled because of the previous problem-solving activity. As ability increases, so does capability; hence, the level of difficulty of new reading problems can be increased. New patterns, meters, and note values are the dimensions of this increasing difficulty.

This structure very conveniently culminates in an easily observed skill behavior. In fact, it may be valuable to have learners check the objective. They could evaluate their performance against a master tape performance that would be supplied them when they were ready to complete the project. This activity would mix skill and perceptive behaviors at the terminal level. Close examination of the various levels leading to the criterion performance reveals many prerequisite cognitive, psychomotor, and perceptual abilities. The learner must know several symbols, terms, and specific bits of knowledge in order to perform accurately. It is interesting to note that a teacher could easily train nine-year-olds to perform a half-dozen rhythm patterns correctly without their knowing anything about music reading. This would be a lower-level chaining performance and could be triggered by visual stimuli in the form of wild African animals. Unfortunately, for years mechanistic rote training has been a trademark of music education. It is really time to teach by sequence for the development of behaviors that will contribute to musical understanding and literacy.

The rhythmic reading learning structure in Figure 5.5 is spread out over a period of several school years. Many of S_s-R first-level experiences, such as body motion in twos and threes, are common kindergarten or first-grade music objectives. Keeping time to steady pulses in musical excerpts is an equally well-known first-year objective in music. The instructional problem is to see that no steps are missed in the total task sequence. First-, second-, and third-year musical training will contain experiences that contribute to the achievement of the rhythmic reading objective as stated. Naturally, there will be other principles and behaviors identified as learning objectives during the same period of musical growth. Many of these other objectives identified will be served by experiences designated as important to the rhythmic reading structure. Undoubtedly there would be overlapping and repetition, but neither one is a source for concern. Almost all duplication of coincident learning would be reinforcing and complementary. Briefly, the structure in terms of child growth might be:

1. Almost all of the S_s-R's and some of the chains are kindergarten learnings. Probably more important early behavioral gains would be positive attitudes toward music and music learning.
2. Many first-grade music experiences and objectives would include the chains indicated in the rhythmic reading structure.
3. Second- and third-grade achievement would include verbal associations and the strengthening of chains.
4. Multiple discriminations through the principle level would be appropriate fourth-grade achievements.

As a learning structure used only in the third or fourth year of elementary general music, the rhythmic reading behavior might well be a self-contained set of experiences. All necessary experiences and achievement could be accomplished in one school year. An unusual amount of cooperation among music teachers, administrators, and classroom teachers would be necessary.

The development of a series of learning structures built on prescribed program objectives is one method of dealing with the instructional sequence problem. Perhaps there are other more convenient methods. Some teachers prefer to identify program objectives and isolate a recognizable sequence of instructional objectives that eventuate in the ability identified in the program objectives. Conductors of performing ensembles who pursue nonperforming objectives, such as cognitive awareness of forms, would need to tie the learning sequence very closely to the repertoire being studied. The identification of experiences appropriate to a learning sequence in a performing group will also vary by the level of ability present and the nature of the medium. Finally, there is some research evidence to indicate that sequence identification is not the crucial problem that it was once believed to be. Learners seem to achieve well if given an objective regardless of what instructional path is followed as long as it has an inherent logical organization.

With the principles of sequencing clearly in mind, the curriculum developer can turn to the organization of learning packages based on program objectives. Each program objective can be broken down into a learning structure by carefully analyzing the necessary mental and motor processes necessary for achievement. These processes become the basis for instructional objectives which, when sequenced accordingly, should produce the capability identified in the program objective. A collection of instructional objectives, with plans for their implementation and evaluation, is termed a learning package. A series of learning packages would, of course, be necessary for each class in the music curriculum reflecting the program objectives for that class. Learning packages would then be the building blocks of the curriculum as illustrated in Figure 5.6.

PRECISE INSTRUCTIONAL PLANNING

Following the identification of an instructional sequence, what remains is day-to-day planning and achievement of a series of instructional objectives. If the teacher follows an instructional map, he should know where the milestones are and what he should be doing as he goes along. The precise nature of learning experiences must be delineated. Instead of reverting to the old lesson-plan idea, a more convenient and free form of daily plan might be used. A copy of the instructional module form is reproduced in Figure 5.7. There is nothing sacred about this form. It has been used successfully by many teachers but there are many other possibilities available. The module represents a specific quantity of instructional time. It may be twenty minutes or several class periods, depending on the nature of the learning experiences and objective. An instructor may not need thirty modules for thirty class periods. Conversely, he may well have from twelve to fifteen modules for ten instructional periods. This is a crucial point. One module is not necessarily one class period. In most cases, however, one module would represent one instructional objective. The largest space on the module form is used to describe the experience or experiences and activities necessary for the achievement of one phase of a specified musical topic. As noted earlier, the learning topic is the generator of the structure and the experience identified is thought to be germane to the pursuit of a course objective. This area of the form is used to define the learning experience, not to delineate methodology. There is no place for methodological preference on the module form. Each teacher is free to pursue a method peculiar to his own ability. If students are developing a capability to discriminate among various ca-

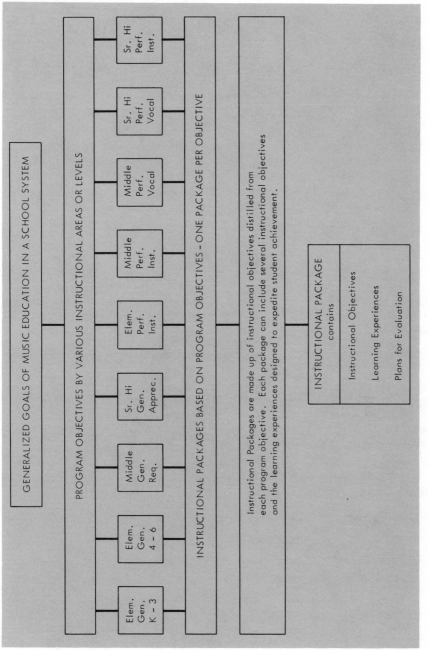

GENERALIZED GOALS OF MUSIC EDUCATION IN A SCHOOL SYSTEM

PROGRAM OBJECTIVES BY VARIOUS INSTRUCTIONAL AREAS OR LEVELS

| Elem. Gen. K – 3 | Elem. Gen. 4 – 6 | Middle Gen. Req. | Sr. Hi Gen. Apprec. | Elem. Perf. Inst. | Middle Perf. Inst. | Middle Perf. Vocal | Sr. Hi Perf. Vocal | Sr. Hi Perf. Inst. |

INSTRUCTIONAL PACKAGES BASED ON PROGRAM OBJECTIVES – ONE PACKAGE PER OBJECTIVE

Instructional Packages are made up of instructional objectives distilled from each program objective. Each package can include several instructional objectives and the learning experiences designed to expedite student achievement.

INSTRUCTIONAL PACKAGE
contains

Instructional Objectives

Learning Experiences

Plans for Evaluation

FIGURE 5.6

MUSIC EXPERIENCE INSTRUCTIONAL MODULE

\# _____

Program Component

LEVEL

Elementary_____ Performance_____ Instrumental_____ General music_____
Secondary_____ Nonperformance_____ Vocal_____ Musicianship_____

Experience Module: (What is the nature of the experience and how will it
                     be conducted?)

Special material required: Titles_____   Number of student
                                                        clock hours needed
Film_____ Transparency _____   to complete this
                                                        module? _____
Recording_____ Video_____

Musical hardware_____

Instruction setting

Large group_____ Small group_____ Independent_____ Other_____

Objective(s):   (Stated in behavior terms, what is this experience designed to
                accomplish?)

Cognitive _____

Affective _____

Psychomotor _____

Prerequisites: (What are the most important two or three competencies needed
                 before working on this objective(s)?)

Evaluation: (What will test whether or not standards of criteria for the success
              of this objective have been reached?)

FIGURE 5.7   MUSIC EXPERIENCE INSTRUCTIONAL MODULE

dences, practice in listening and labeling cadences can be accomplished in many ways. Many strategies should probably be employed but the exact nature or order of performance, listening, or creating is a teacher's decision. The objective and experiences can best be served by the teacher doing what he does best. Rigid procedures must not be imposed. Nevertheless, individual teachers may have very specific approaches from which they do not wish to deviate. It may well be helpful to record successful approaches for any new teacher working in the system in the future. These would only form a group of suggested procedures. In performance teaching particularly, music teachers are aware of the need for many approaches and strategies in order to combat individual differences and problems. The nature of the learning experience must be very carefully described on the module. The manner of presentation does not have to be noted at all. The quality of the experience is foremost; therefore, the teacher must be free to operate in his most secure manner. The kind of students and the nature of their involvement should be described. The final considerations for the quality of the experience are those of media and musical hardware. Appropriate films, filmstrips, recordings, and their locations should be designated. Necessary musical equipment, such as rhythm instruments or acoustical equipment should be detailed. The purpose is, of course, to provide teachers with every aid to successful instruction. The following experiences were designated for the first three class meetings of an introductory course in music:

Session I 1. Clap, tap, chant pulse and rhythms using dictated patterns of poem rhythms.

2. Read poems in groups.

3. Move to rhythms of poems.

4. Step pulse while reciting word patterns.

5. As a group, intone poems that have strict pulses.
Objective: Given word rhythms from poems, the learner can tap pulse while chanting, clapping, or tah-ing the implied pattern.

Session II 1. Review motor responses from Session I.

2. Discuss time values and their rests (limited values).

3. Sing a known song that has note and rest values studied; clap the pulse.

4. Read patterns of note values learned.

5. Using only rhythmic sounds, create consequent phrase to given stem.

6. Rote dictation drills; echo clapped stimulus.
Objective: Given visual (to read) or aural (to imitate) rhythmic patterns, the learner can clap, chant, tap, or tah while maintaining a steady pulse.

Session III 1. Review material from Sessions I and II.
  2. Write note and rest chart for values studied.
  3. Using values studied, take dictation of rhythmic patterns.
  4. Using values studied, improvise and compose rhythm patterns.
  5. Listen to selected recording in which note values and patterns used are those studied (Beethoven, Symphony No. 7, Second Movement).
  Objective: Same as in Session II.

Restrictions of space do not permit a full detailed sequence of the experiences. The above examples represent learning experiences appropriate to the objectives for the first three instructional sessions. Obviously, the objectives deal with rhythmic notation, pulse, and durational sound/silence symbols.

Another important area on the module form is space for the instructional staff to enter the objective of the experience. It should be noted that all precautions of good objective writing still hold. The statement should be in behavioral terms and describe *exactly* what the experience is designed to accomplish. Any reader should know what the target of instruction is. If the experience deals with presenting certain durational values to learners, the objective might well call for discrimination between pairs of notes presented aurally or visually. Several modules could have the same objective if the experiences were varied but were all part of one small bit of learning. More often each module will have several recommended experiences leading to a single objective that will take two or three class periods. The objective is also identified according to the kind of music learning involved: cognitive, affective, or psychomotor. These designations are only a matter of convenience.

The curriculum developer in music education should think comprehensively about the kinds of learning experiences he offers learners. One means of classifying learning experiences is depicted in Figure 5.8. Given an elemental approach to music, one can identify the kind of interaction with the desired type of resultant behavior—affective, cognitive, or psychomotor. Each of these dimensions is fixed to be coincident with a musical element. Such a view of learning experiences can allow the teacher to be eclectic and comprehensive in selecting learning experiences. This insures achievement by all kinds of learners because each student can learn effectively in different ways. The teacher should not constrain himself to one approach for all learning. Neither should one methodology rule. Given the three basic kinds of pupil interaction with music, a vast thesaurus of learner experiences is identifiable.

There are two important categories on the module form yet to be discussed: prerequisites and evaluation. The writer of the module should enter in the prerequisite space the most important one, two, or three

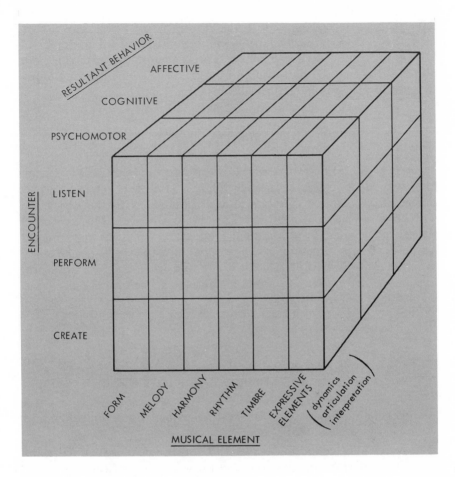

FIGURE 5.8

competencies or experiences needed before working on the present objective. This is a precautionary procedure to ensure smooth instructional flow and allow for differences in learners. Again, this statement is couched in behavioral terms.

The purpose of evaluation is to detail what will measure whether or not the student has achieved the objective of the module. The statement may be in the form of a test question or merely a specific kind of behavior that the teacher should look for in the learners either collectively or individually. Evaluation is essential to good curriculum planning because it is the source for further refinement and redevelopment of instructional programs. If the module shows no way of knowing whether or not an objective has been reached, a teacher cannot determine the effectiveness of a particular learning experience. Accurate information for measurement purposes must be included when a program of learning experiences is planned. The results of the evaluation can also shed light on the contribution of the module to the program objective and its instructional sequence.

SUMMARY

Music education programs are in need of precise instructional planning. The identification of learning topics is a necessary step in this procedure. Once a topic is identified as a program objective, the instruction staff can prescribe a sequence of learning experiences. This process is termed *task analysis*. The resultant sequence becomes the basis for experiences in music that have real purpose to course or program objectives. Sequence is directly related to how and when children can learn. Experiences are simply confrontations (listening, performing, and creating) learners have with music.

QUESTIONS FOR STUDY OR DISCUSSION

1. Prepare a tentative learning structure for the First-Year Objective for beginning wind players.
2. Select a dozen common musical behaviors you demonstrate and list prerequisite abilities for each.
3. Write a fifteen-module plan for teaching an instrumental or choral performing group a unit on serial composition.
4. What is the first behavior that beginning violinists should acquire? Indicate a precise sequence for ensuring that the behavior is securely learned.
5. Develop a learning sequence for junior-high general music classes. What information would be advantageous at the beginning?
6. List ten simple forms of musical behavior and relate them to Gagné's learning hierarchy.

SUPPLEMENTARY READINGS

Ausubel, David, *The Psychology of Meaningful Verbal Learning.* New York: Grune & Stratton, Inc., 1963.

Bruner, Jerome, *The Process of Education*. Cambridge: Harvard University Press, 1960.

DeCecco, J. P., *Educational Technology*. New York: Holt, Rinehart and Winston, Inc., 1964.

French, Will, *Behavioral Goals of General Education*. New York: Russell Sage Foundation, 1957.

Oliver, Albert I., *Curriculum Improvement*. New York: Dodd, Mead & Co., 1965.

Taba, Hilda, *Curriculum Development: Theory and Practice*. New York: Harcourt, Jovanovich Inc., 1962.

CHAPTER SIX

evaluation:
student and program

All writers in the field of curriculum stress the importance of evaluation as a continuing part of the curriculum development process. In order to evaluate the effectiveness of the instructional system, student competence must be measured at the terminal point of instruction. It is through student evaluation that decisions regarding the modification of the instructional program become possible. Are objectives being met? Can learners perform what they are asked? Are expected outcomes realistic? What steps must be taken to increase the efficiency of the instructional system? All of these questions need answers if long-term goals of music education are going to be met. In addition, there is a need to look among potential music learners for individual differences in both capability and learning style. Those of outstanding talent should be identified and led to find more challenging experiences in school music.

Two types of measurement lead to a complete plan of evaluation for the music program. The first relates mainly to the instructional program. Students are measured and subsequently evaluated according to locally developed objectives. These objectives are of the program type, specific and clear communicators of instructional intent. Measuring student competence in relation to these objectives is classified as criterion-referenced measurement. Clearly stated program objectives contain statements of acceptable performance levels which form the criteria for the outcome indicated.

The purpose of this type of measurement is to assess the effectiveness of the instructional system in bringing about the learning intended. If learners cannot do what is asked as a result of the instructional program, some modification is clearly in order.

The second type of measurement is termed norm-referenced measurement. The purpose is quite different from that of criterion-referenced testing. The purpose of norm-referenced testing is to discover differences among students in accumulated musical ability and talent, or to find the most suitable learning style. For example, the use of a standardized achievement test prior to beginning music instruction in the middle school would indicate various levels of musical capability among students. Some students would display high achievement and others low. The purpose is to uncover differences among students; hence the process is classified as norm-referenced testing.

Both kinds of measurement have a place in the overall evaluative phase of the curriculum development process. Banathy states that, "tests are designed for the purpose of:

—Measuring the input competence of the learner in relation to the learning task to be attempted.

—Measuring the degree to which the learner has the competences that are prerequisite to mastering learning tasks.

—Diagnosing learning style and learning rate so as to best accommodate the individual.

—Assessing the progress of the learner in order to introduce changes that will enable him to perform in the expected way.

—Pointing toward specific deficiencies in the system itself.[1]

In another way, the measurement problem facing music educators is unique among educational assessment. Roughly, 15% of the music program can be measured by giving written tests. Another 20% must include the use of aural stimuli in the measurement exercise, since listening perception must be a cornerstone of musical competence. At least 40 percent of what should be evaluated in music is in the nature of perform-

---

[1] Bela Banathy, *Instruction Systems* (Palo Alto: Fearon Publishers, 1968), p. 81.

ance from gross to very refined levels of motor activity. Finally, the importance of attitude and appreciation assessment cannot be overstressed; presently it suffers from inadequate procedures for evaluation. The complexity of the evaluation problem for the music education staff is almost overwhelming but not insurmountable if the staff commits itself to attacking the problem and finding creative solutions.

NORM-REFERENCED MUSIC ACHIEVEMENT TESTS

One approach to assessing student background is to use published tests. There is, however, a paucity of standardized tests available for the measurement of musical achievement. The few extant tests assess both verbal and aural music phenomena. By and large, these tests are most valuable in assessing *general* levels of music knowledge and perception. What they measure is not likely to be totally appropriate to the objectives defined by any specific school system or a particular instructional sequence. Nevertheless, published tests are likely to be more objective and enjoy development at the hands of expert test-makers. Being standardized, the tests offer a composite of carefully selected items which have been shaped into the best form by a long process of trial administration, development, and sophisticated field testing. Appropriate statistical analyses of the tests provide valuable data for purposes of comparison. The abilities of local students can be compared with performances by a large national, standardizing sample of students. If prudently used, published tests can also help estimate entry behavior levels. However, it would be foolish to use a test that did not measure, at least in a general way, local objectives. It is very useful to assess the extent of student ability in music prior to instruction. As noted above, such data can assist in individualizing the instructional process. The results of an entering test can be used to solve individual difference problems and determine the most appropriate beginning level for all students starting an instructional continuum. If a learner already shows acceptable behavior, there is no need for him to go through the learning sequence. For students with less experience, a remedial instructional program or allowance for tutorial help may be appropriate.

The following short list of achievement tests includes those which would be available for system-wide testing and may conceivably function as course pre-tests in some cases.

1. *Achievement Tests in Music,* "Recognition of Rhythm and Melody," William A. Knuth (Monmouth, Oregon: Creative Arts Research Asso-

ciates, 1967. Division I, II, III and Forms A and B. The student hears a performance of complete musical phrases and is asked to indicate the error between notation and aural stimuli. Uses a filmstrip and audio tape. Norms are from 1932.

2. *Music Achievement Tests,* Richard Colwell (Chicago: Follett Education Corporation, 1968–69). Thirty-six pages. Administrative and scoring manuals for Tests 1 and 2, a 143-page interpretive manual for the combined tests. Comparable manuals for Tests 3 and 4. *Test I:* Pitch Discrimination; Interval Discrimination; Meter Discrimination. *Test II:* (1) Auditory-Visual Discrimination; (2) Tonal Center; (3) Major-minor Discrimination. *Test III:* (1) Tonal Memory; (2) Melody Recognition; (3) Pitch Recognition; (4) Instrument Recognition. *Test IV:* (1) Style; (2) Texture; (3) Auditory/Visual Rhythm; (4) Chord Recognition.

3. *Snyder-Knuth Music Achievement Test* (Monmouth, Oregon: Cara Publications, 1968). Forms A and B, 7-page manual. There are two forms, each having four parts: listening and seeing, listening, musical comprehension, and tonal memory.

4. *Aliferis Music Achievement Test,* James Aliferis (Minneapolis: University of Minnesota Press, 1954). (Distributed by Harcourt, Brace Jovanovich, Inc.). 28-page manual. Three subtests—rhythm, melody, and harmony—designed to assess the capabilities of entering college freshmen. The test is administered at the piano or on tape.

5. *Iowa Tests of Music Literacy,* Edwin Gordon (Iowa City: to be published by the University of Iowa). Measures musical achievement in the areas of tonal and rhythmic aural perception, reading recognition, and notational understanding. Six concepts are measured in each of six test levels.

There are other music achievement tests, but they are severely out of date. Advances in measurement practice, test design, and item analysis leave room for revision of older tests.

Music achievement can also take the form of instrumental or vocal performance. There are few published tests dealing with this form of musical behavior. Perhaps the best known is the *Watkins-Farnum Performance Scale*[2] that was designed to measure musical achievement for all band instruments. Performers sight read musical examples and the judge records errors in performance capabilities. A more recent test is the *Farnum String Scale,*[3] for which only limited data on its effectiveness are available at this time. Performance tests can be used to place performers in large ensembles and to test sight-reading ability. When they are used

---

[2] John Watkins and Stephen Farnum, *The Watkins–Farnum Performance Scale* (Winona, Minn.: The Hal Leonard Music Co., 1954).

[3] John Farnum, *The Farnum String Scale* (Winona, Minn.: The Hal Leonard Music Co., 1969).

for tryouts and seating, they function as a pre-test for assessing entry behaviors of performers.

NORM-REFERENCED ATTITUDE AND
APPRECIATION MEASURES

Standardized tests of attitudes and appreciations are also rare. Naturally, measurement of these activities is extremely difficult because of the severe restrictions nonverbal behaviors impose. Current research and development of evaluation tools for affective objectives promises some aid for this difficult area of measurement. Among others, the work of Kyme,[4] Colwell,[5] and Long[6] is particularly noteworthy. Music educators are often satisfied to claim that what they teach is not measurable. This viewpoint has undoubtedly led to the shortage of music attitude and appreciation measures. Furthermore, their "head in the sand" position leaves the music educator teaching something that he admits does not measurably alter an individual's behavior. A brief list of available measures includes:

1. *Oregon Music Discrimination Test,* Kate Hevner (Chicago: C. A. Stoelting Company, 1935).
2. *Tests of Melodic and Harmonic Sensitivity,* J. Kwalwassar (Camden, N.J.: The Victor Talking Machine Co., 1926).
3. *Revision of Oregon Music Discrimination Test,* Newell Long (U.S. Office of Education, 1965).

CRITERION-REFERENCED TEACHER-MADE TESTS

Although the advantages of nationwide objectives and tests designed for them are many, local music staffs must develop instructional systems appropriate to their local community. Using only standardized tests is a tacit acceptance of someone else's objectives. Furthermore, norm-oriented testing is likely to be unacceptable in many communities. With the development of statement of accurate local instructional and program ob-

---

[4] George Kyme, "The Value of Aesthetic Judgments in the Assessment of Musical Capacity" (unpublished Ph.D. dissertation, The University of California, Berkeley, 1954).

[5] Richard Colwell, "Music Education and Experiment Research," *Journal of Research in Music Education,* vol. 15, no. 1 (Spring, 1967), 73.

[6] Newell Long, "A Revision of the University of Oregon Music Discrimination Test" (unpublished Ed.D. dissertation, Indiana University, 1965).

jectives, measurement and evaluation problems are significantly reduced. Very likely the most perplexing measurement problem is to determine what should be tested. Nevertheless, when objectives have been formulated, the targets of measurement are clearly defined. The only decision remaining is the strategy for measurement. Is the process to be written testing, subjective monitoring, or nondirective observation of behavior? Naturally, decisions on the form of measurement must be made in relation to stated objectives for various learning structures. Students need these evaluations in order to provide reinforcement for what has been learned and motivation for additional development of capabilities. Provision should be made to provide students with immediate feedback of their test performances with appropriate evaluation statements of what they can do to improve.

Teachers who develop tests in order to assess achievement of local objectives should keep in mind two important characteristics of good measures. There are many other considerations but the following are mentioned most often by writers in the measurement field:

1. *A test should be reliable.* Test reliability implies accuracy and consistency of measurement. When a test is reliable, an individual will achieve approximately the same score on repeated administrations.
2. *A test should be valid.* Test validity implies assurance that it does, in fact, measure what it is supposed to measure. Of particular importance in this regard is the degree of coincidence between test content and program objective content. Things measured must be things taught.

Teacher-made tests usually achieve relatively moderate levels of reliability. Pupils should perform about as well one day as the next on a well-structured teacher-made test. Correlating two test performances by the same group of students provides about the best check of reliability for a locally developed test. Teachers should be able to secure assistance in estimating the reliability of their tests by supervisory or research personnel in the school system.

Validity of local tests is best determined by empirically matching test items or exercises to the objectives supposedly being measured. The accuracy of content is the prime concern and items which do not precisely reflect objectives should be cast out.

One final dimension of test construction is important in criterion-referenced measurement. The purpose of this kind of test is to assess the effectiveness of an instructional system. If the instructional system has been effective, all learners should correctly answer all test items, if said items are valid in content to the instructional or program objectives. Such a pattern of response will lead to very low difficulty levels for each item. The difficulty level of a test item is the percentage of learners missing or omitting the item. Low difficulty indices for test items would indicate that most learners are correctly responding. This outcome, is, of course, what the developer of an instructional systems is looking for—high achievement levels for most of his students.

NATURE OF TEST CONTENT

Cognitive, perceptual, and some affective behaviors are often measured by written tests. Facts important to the musical symbol system, historical data, verbal concepts, and principles of music constitute a body of information which is also often tested this way. Test items include multiple choice, matching, and other well-known objective exercises. These items are efficient for checking recall of knowledge bits. More sophisticated verbal behaviors about music can be assessed by giving essay questions that require analysis, synthesis, and evaluation level abilities by learners. Perceptual skills are well appraised by learner response to recorded or live performed musical excerpts. Items on aural tests often call for discrimination, differentiation, and identification behaviors by learners. A great amount of aural experience and subsequent aural measurement is a hallmark of effective programs in music education. Murphy has written, "listening is undeniably the sole basis of musical experience."[7] Measures of perceptive listening should include test experiences in which the student is asked to identify, label, or describe specific musical events. This can be done while the student listens to a complete music selection of short duration. In other words, the test experience is precisely the same as a true music listening experience. Written tests may also be employed to appraise student attitudes toward music as well as individual preferences and values. Characteristically, these measures use items that require the examinee to circle preferences along a like to dislike continuum.

Performance testing is usually accomplished on an individual basis. If performance objectives are precisely defined, the evaluator's role is greatly simplified. Figure 6.1 shows a skills achievement card for freshmen nonmusic majors. It is used to record performance behavior levels of elementary education majors. Achievement is recorded on the grade scales used for term evaluations. The continuum moves from simple to complex behaviors in five areas. Learners play, sing, or tap various harmonic, melodic, and rhythmic material. Playing performance can be on

---

[7] Howard Murphy, *Teaching Musicianship* (New York: Coleman-Ross Co., 1950), p. 60.

any instrument for almost all levels. When the course begins, learners are provided with a copy of the verbal descriptions of behaviors on each level (see the outline on pp. 126–128). Students are free to try any level in sequence at any time during the term. Both student and teacher keep track of achievement at various levels and reinforcement is immediate. The spaces on the card contain shorthand statements of performance behaviors. Similar evaluative tools could be developed for music study on any level as long as objectives that clearly described performance behaviors were available. An evaluation tool for some primary performance skills in the elementary school is on page 129.[8]

Directors of instrumental and choral performance groups would be wise to define performance skills and expectations more carefully. Statements describing entry abilities and terminal performance levels could add greatly to the educational contribution of large ensembles. Even more valuable would be the learners' awareness of what they should achieve and whether or not they have achieved it.

Other assessment tools that can shed important evidence on the achievement of affective goals in music education are nonreactive or unobtrusive measures. In most cases, measurement is made without directly confronting those who are being measured. Typically, little or no cooperation is needed from subjects. The following is a very short list of possible approaches:

1. Keep a record of instrument and music checked out to take home.
2. Keep a log of materials checked out of the library.
3. Check rate of page wear in certain library reference books.
4. Check organization rolls for level of community interest in music.
5. Keep a record of who attends concerts.
6. Tape-record lessons and rehearsals.
7. Eavesdrop on intermission conversations.
8. Check records bought and/or owned by students.
9. Make a survey of students' TV preferences.

On pages 130–132 there is a nine-unit instructional package developed by Charles Hills of the Ann Arbor Public Schools.[9] Students tape-record each unit when ready. Feedback is provided by the teacher in the form of the accompanying evaluation sheet. Students can move through the sequence at their own pace. The nine-unit package is designed to fit into a single semester at the seventh-grade level.

---

[8] Kay Melton, "Music Progress Report" (unpublished documents, 1971).
[9] Charles Hills, *7th Grade Cadet Band Assignment Sheets*, unpublished document, Ann Arbor, Michigan, February, 1972.

Evaluation of Music Performance Skills

Level	Rhythm	Level	Melody	Level	Harmony
A	4/4, [rhythm notation] Dictated, student echoes 2 bars,	A	5 finger tunes, prepared, 3/4, 4/4, keys G,F,C [melody notation]	A	Given letter name, play major or minor triad, root position
B	3/4 Dictated, student echoes 2 bars	B	Octave range, prepared tune, (MM = 60) [melody notation]	B	Given letter C,F,G play triad M-m or m-M
C	Four bars, student reads	C	Sight read, add key of D (MM = 72) [melody notation]	C	Prepared song (MM = 72) keys CFG, chords IVI, piano, autoharp
D	6/8, [rhythm notation]	D	Sight read, add key of A Syncopation, small leaps of 3rd [melody notation]	D	Prepared chords I, IV, V_7, keys of CFGDA —no written symbols
E	Syncopation [rhythm notation]	E	Expanded octave range, larger skips Bb,Eb [melody notation]	E	Play Block Chord Accompaniment to new melody—Add Bb,Eb

Playing

124

Singing

Level	Rhythm	Level	Melody	Level	Harmony
F	5/4 and changing meters	F	All keys [musical notation]	F	New melody, differing meters, differing accompaniment styles
		A	Sing 5-3 pattern, own range	A	Own range, major triad
		B	m3rd, 7 note pattern by sight end on 1	B	Sing roots of I, IV, V, I
		C	pentatonic, four bars, 4/4, 3/4, 2/4 [musical notation]	C	Triads in progression, I, V, I Keys, C, F, G
		D	Major, scalewise, 4 bars, [musical notation]	D	Triads in progression I, IV, V, I, Keys C, F, G
		E	Diatonic Intervals 8 measures [musical notation]	E	Chord roots with song from instructor, I,IV,V_7, D, A, Bb,E-flat
		F	Changing meters, all keys	F	Triads, I, vi, IV, ii, V_7, I

NAME _____

Section _____ Term _____

Skills Achievement Score

FIGURE 6.1

125

PERFORMANCE OBJECTIVES

I. Playing: Rhythm

    A. Given a dictated two-measure, nonpitched rhythm pattern, the learner can precisely imitate by clapping, tapping, or "tahing" after one hearing. Meter will be 4/4; tempo ♩ = 76 and sound silence symbols will include quarter, half, and eighth notes and quarter and eighth rests. (No errors permitted.)

    B. Given a dictated two-measure, nonpitched rhythm pattern, the learner can precisely imitate by clapping, tapping, or "tahing" after one hearing. Meter will be 3/4 or 4/4. Tempo and sound silence patterns values the same as in objective A. (No errors.)

    C. Given a printed four-measure, nonpitched rhythm pattern, the learner can tap, "tah," or clap it at sight without error. Meter, tempo, and sound/silence values as in No. B level.

    D. Given a printed four-measure, nonpitched rhythm pattern, the learner can tap, "tah," or clap it without error at sight. Meter can be 3/4, 4/4, 6/8; tempo ♩ = 76. Sound/silence patterns those of B level plus ♫♫, ♩, ♪, ♩, 𝅝 .

    E. Given a printed four-measure, nonpitched rhythm pattern, the learner can tap, "tah," or clap it without error at sight. Meter and tempo the same as O. Additional sound/silence patterns to include ♩. ♫, ♪♩ ♪ and ♫♫ .

    F. Precisely the same as E level with addition of 5/4 meter and changing meters 2/4, 3/4, 4/4, 5/4, 6/8, 5/8, 5/16, 2/8, 3/8.

II. Playing: Melody

    A. Play at a keyboard instrument a prepared tune in 3/4 or 4/4 meter at a steady tempo. Keys will be C, F, and G. Sound/silence patterns to include ♩, ♫, ♩, 𝄽 . Compass of the melody will not exceed the interval of a fifth. The learner may have two opportunities to be tested for this objective in a term. Two attempts are allowed in each testing. Minimum errors are two in pitch and two in rhythm.

    B. Play at a keyboard instrument a prepared tune at a tempo of ♩ = 60. Meters and keys the same as A level. Sound/silence include those at the A level plus ♩. ♪ and 𝄾 Compass of the melody should be an octave.

    C. Given a melodic excerpt, the learner can play it with accuracy the first time at a keyboard instrument. All previous range, patterns, tempi, and keys are appropriate plus:

        Key of D, tempo to ♩ = 72

        Pattern ♫♫ Meter 6/8

D. Given a melodic excerpt, the learner can play it with accuracy the first time at a keyboard instrument. All previous range, pattern, tempi, key, and meter are in effect plus:

Pattern ♪♩ ♪♪♪|♪ Key of A

Also small leaps of a third are appropriate.

E. Given a melodic excerpt, the learner can play it with accuracy the first time at a keyboard instrument. The following determinants are now in effect:

Range: more than an octave, small, and large leaps
Meter: 3/4, 4/4, 6/8, B-flat
Keys: C, F, G, D, A, E-flat

Patterns: ♩. ♩ ♩♪♩ ♪♪♩

Tempo: ♩ = 72

F. Given a melodic excerpt, the learner can play it with accuracy at sight at the keyboard instrument. All determinants of level E plus ♪♪♩♪♩, ♩♪♪♪♪

and all keys.

III. Playing: Harmony

A. Given a letter name, the learner can play at a keyboard instrument a major or minor triad in root position without error.

B. Given the letter C, F, or G, the learner can play and transform a triad from major to minor or minor to major without error.

C. The learner can prepare and play accurately at the piano a simple tune that can be harmonized with I and V chords. Appropriate list is available. Keys C, F, G. ("Go Tell Aunt Rhody," "Skip to My Lou," "Go Tell It on the Mountain" are examples.)

D. The learner can prepare and perform at the piano a simple tune that can be harmonized by I, IV, V_7 chords. Keys are C, F, G, D, A. There are to be no written chord symbols. ("Silent Night," "Auld Lang Syne.")

E. Given an unknown melody with chord symbols, the learner can play a block-style accompaniment at sight, without error. Keys C, F, G, D, A, B-flat, E-flat.

F. Given an unknown melody without chord symbols, the learner can play with *Alberti*, stride, or block accompaniment (as directed) at sight. There will be changing or unusual meters.

IV. Singing: Melody

A. The learner is able to sing a descending minor third in a comfortable range.

B. Given nonmusical symbols of a seven-note melodic pattern, the learner can sing without error on sight

5 3 5 3 3 5 1
5 3 5 5 3 3 1
5 3 3 3 5 3 1

C. Given visually notated pentatonic melodic excerpts of four bars, the learner can sing without error on the second try. Meters can be 4/4, 3/4, or 2/4. Sound patterns of ♩, ♫, ♩. .

D. Given visually a notated diatonic melody of four bars, the learner can sing without error on the second try. The melody will include sound/silence symbols of level C plus the quarter rest, and it will be scalewise in character.

E. Given visually a notated diatonic melody of eight bars, the learner can sing without error on the second try. New dimensions include all diatonic intervals and the following new rhythm patterns: ♩. ♪, ♬♬, ♩. ♪ .

F. Given visually a notated melody of eight bars or more, the learner can sing without error on the second try. Previous dimensions are in effect together with all and changing meters and any key signature.

V. Singing: Harmony

A. The learner is able to sing a descending m3 in his own voice range.

B. The learner is able to sing a major triad in your voice range on the first try. You may choose the starting pitch.

C. The learner is able to sing the chord progression I, V, I; letter names in your range on the first try. Keys: C, F, G.

D. The learner is able to sing roots of chords I, IV, V in your own range while examiner plays or sings an appropriate tune. You will have two tries to succeed.

E. Given a key, the learner can sing the chord progression I, IV, V_7, I using letter names without error. Keys of C, G, D, A, F, B-flat, E-flat.

F. Given a key, the learner can sing the chord progression, I, vi, ii, IV, V_7, I using letter names without error. Keys the same as level E.

MUSIC PROGRESS REPORT

_____

name

RHYTHM
  Steady Beat
  Echo Clap with teacher
  Clap Note Values
  Rhythm Sheets
  Auto-harp Accompaniment

SINGING
  Match Pitches with Teacher
  Sing Melodies
  Sing Harmony Part

MUSIC READING
  Basic Terms
  Clefs
  Music Signs

LISTENING
  Call Charts
  Indentifies Instruments

PARTICIPATION
  and Attitudes

key: S-Superior A-Average N-Needs Improvement U-Unsatisfactory

Parents Signature:

1st period

2nd period

3rd period

4th period

Used in the Eaton Rapids Elementary Schools, Eaton Rapids, Michigan.

TAPPAN JUNIOR HIGH SCHOOL
ANN ARBOR, MICHIGAN
Seventh Grade Cadet Band

Instructional Material*

UNIT I

B-flat scale pattern—slurred.

Exercise 9, page 4
  Set metronome at 144 (1 tick per eighth note).
  Tap your foot audibly (2 metronome ticks per foot tap).
  Hold note values for proper number of ticks, stopping on last tick of
    each note.

Exercise 16, page 5   *Drums:* 1. B-flat scale on Bells. Set
  Set metronome at 144.   metronome at 144.
  Tap foot audibly.
  Release notes on the last tick.
  Beware of the rests.

UNIT II

E-flat scale pattern—slurred.   *Drums:* 1. Paradiddles (single) No. 2.

Exercise 9, page 7   2. Flamacue No. 5.
  MM = 144; tap foot audibly.   3. Chromatic scale on Bells.
Exercise 15   Quarter notes. Set metro-
  MM = 160; tap foot audibly.   nome at 144.
  4 measures on a breath.
  Legato (connected) style.

Exercise 17, page 9
  MM = 160
  Staccato (detached, separated) style. Release on last tick.
  8 measures to a breath. Breathe on last tick before breath mark.
  B-flat concert chromatic scale—one octave; 5-note pattern—slurred.

UNIT III

F concert scale pattern—slurred.   *Drums:* 1. Flamaddidle No. 2.

Exercise 9, page 10   2. Tympani—F–B-flat tuning.
  MM = 160; tap foot audibly.   3. Special Problems C, page
Exercise 11, page 11   10.
  MM = 144; 4 measures in one breath.
  Legato (connected) style.

---

* From Fred Weber, *Belwin Intermediate Band Method,* published by Belwin-
Mills, Inc.

Exercise 17, page 12, "America, the Beautiful"
8 measures in one breath.
Legato style.

UNIT IV

A-flat scale pattern—slurred.

Exercise 8, page 13
MM = 116; eighth note equals one tick; tap foot.

Exercise 9, page 13
MM = 116; eighth note equals one tick; tap foot.

Exercise 12, page 14
MM = 116; eighth note equals one tick; watch special articulations; four-measure breaths.

Exercise 15, page 14
MM = 120; eighth note equals one tick; tap foot; four-measure breaths; connected style.

Exercise 17, page 15
MM = 120; eighth note equals one tick; eight-measure breath; connected style.

UNIT V

A-flat, B-flat, E-flat, and F patterns in sequence.

Exercise 13, page 17
Detached style; four-measure breaths; MM = 132; eighth note equals one tick.

Exercise 14, page 17
Cut time; four-measure breaths; detached style; MM = 132; quarter note equals one tick.

Exercise 15, page 17
Four-measure breaths, staccato style, MM = 144; eighth note equals one tick.

Exercise 18, page 18
Four-measure phrase; use foot tap, no metronome; staccato style.

UNIT VI

C scale pattern—slurred.

Exercise 9, page 19
Use only foot tap.

Exercise 14, page 20
Legato style; four-measure breaths; MM = 120; eighth note equals one tick.

Exercise 15, page 20
Staccato style; four-measure breaths, MM = 144; eighth note equals one tick.

Exercise 17, page 21
Breaths as marked; use only foot tap; legato style.

B-flat chromatic scale pattern—foot tap.

UNIT VII

Exercise 11
  Set metronome at 176–200 = one note of a triplet; breathe every four
    bars only.
Exercise 12
  Set metronome at 176–200 = one note of a triplet; breathe every four
    bars only.
Exercise 18
  "Animal Fair"
Exercise 19
  "Good Bye, My Lover, Good Bye"
  Drums only—add street beat.

UNIT VIII

Exercise 3
  Breathe every two bars only.
Exercise 10
  Second line at 120 = eighth note; be very accurate; breathe every four
    bars only.
Exercise 12
  Set metronome at 132 = eighth note; breathe every *two* bars only.
Exercise 13
  Second line only; set metronome at 144 = eighth note; breathe every
    four bars only.

UNIT IX

Exercise 11
  Breathe every four bars.
Exercise 15
  Breathe every four bars.
Exercise 17
  "Our Boys Will Shine Tonite"
Exercise 19
  "L'il Liza Jane"
  Drums omit 15 and add street beat.

CADET BAND ACHIEVEMENT TEST CRITIQUE

To: _____   Tested on: _____

From: Mr. Hills   Date: _____

You had these problems on this assignment:

Specific suggestions for improvement:

Perhaps the most significant terminal objectives of music education relate to continued life interest in music. This interest is probably best assessed by observing the behaviors of program graduates, who may attend concerts, buy records, financially support music budgets in churches, sing in choirs, perform in amateur or professional music groups, subscribe to music magazines, read newspaper or magazine articles about music events, support local concert series, insist upon music training for their children, choose musical involvement over some other attractive avocational activity. Those who make these decisions are basing them on a set of values about music and its place in their lives. If music education programs produce individuals who exhibit the foregoing behaviors, the instructional program could be making the difference. Local staffs might estimate the percentage of graduates who choose post-school music involvement and the data may be used assess achievement of affective objectives. It would also be valuable to institute a continuing status research project that would provide data relevant to music activity in the community. Finally, and equally worthwhile, a comparative longitudinal study of what graduates of different times have done or supported in music could provide data that reflect the curriculum. These findings furnish tangible evidence for instituting program modifications following careful reevaluation of the curriculum.

CURRICULUM EVALUATION

One writer defines curriculum evaluation as "a comprehensive term relating to the process of inquiry into the adequacy of a school's educational program and the appropriateness of it's curriculum development."[10] Another writer, who is closer to music education, has recently defined curriculum evaluation as a "determination of the status of the program in relation to program objectives of the general philosophy of the program and includes as many facets and factors of the school program as lend themselves to evaluation or can be evaluated with a reasonable degree of time and expense."[11] Oliver sums up the process of the curriculum evaluation by identifying as targets of appraisal:[12]

---

[10] Albert I. Oliver, *Curriculum Improvement* (New York: Dodd, Mead & Co., 1965), p. 379.

[11] Richard J. Colwell, *Evaluation in Music* (Englewood Cliffs, N.J.: Prentice-Hall, Inc., 1970).

[12] Oliver, *op. cit.*, p. 384.

1. *program* (what should be included in the educational program, for whom, and when?);
2. *provisions* (the adequacy of space, equipment, materials);
3. *procedures* (the effectiveness of grouping, of the aural–oral method of language teaching, of democratic classrooms, etc.);
4. *products* (various behaviors of the learner both in and out of the school situation, both now and in the future).

Program evaluation is a process demanding involvement from a number of individuals. Successful change is more assured if the concept of "psychological ownership" is operating. Again, according to Oliver, "a person will more likely accept change if he is involved."[13] Music teachers, classroom teachers, supervisors, administrators, laymen, local professional musicians, and outside consultants could comprise an evaluation team. In addition, perpetual evaluation is necessary for the upkeep of instructional programs. Teachers and learning specialists should constantly be alert for evidence of program success and failure. If students are not successful in achieving objectives, there is no need to wait for an outside evaluation team to come. Isolate the problem and institute another approach quickly. This system of appraisal is possible if during the program development process an evaluation procedure is built into each instructional block. Scrivens[14] calls for both formative and summative evaluation. During the period when materials are being developed to implement objectives they are experimentally tried in actual classroom situations. After reshaping and editing have occurred, the total plan is operative. At this point Scrivens indicates that the summative period of evaluation begins.

WHAT TO EVALUATE

Curriculum evaluation includes the assessment of both process and product. Grobman states that "without evaluation of the process of producing, trying out, and disseminating materials, the project may be defeating its own purpose, since the curriculum problem may be one of better implementation rather than one of more or different materials."[15] Product evaluation deals with assessing student gains and judg-

---

13 *Ibid.*, p. 383.

14 Michael Scriven, "The Methodology of Evaluation," *Perspectives of Curriculum Evaluation* (Chicago: Rand, McNally & Co., 1967), pp. 40–43.

15 Hulda Grobman, *Evaluation Activities of Curriculum Projects: A Starting Point* (Chicago: Rand McNally & Co., 1968), p. 27.

ing the adequacy, relevance, and validity of the learning materials and strategy. The actual process of program evaluation then involves the total investigation of the school's instructional program in music. Leonhard and House[16] describe program evaluation as a three-phase procedure that includes "(1) validation of objectives, (2) collecting data regarding the objectives, and (3) the subsequent interpretation of these data." In addition, there are other aspects of the program that can be the target of the evaluation process. Admittedly, many school programs have not developed all of the following items for the music curriculum or any other field. Nevertheless, an evaluating team should direct its attention to:

1. philosophy of the program;
2. terminal goals;
3. course division and program objectives;
4. content, sequence, and instructional objectives;
5. nature of learning experiences;
6. scheduling and facilities;
7. plans for evaluation.

Careful and complete examination of these seven areas should make it possible to prescribe what changes, if any, are needed to improve the instructional program.

PHILOSOPHY OF THE PROGRAM

The music department of a school system should have a basic philosophic statement on the value of music in education. It may be only a vague assertion, e.g., music is a pleasure-giving activity; nevertheless, the statement serves as a springboard for the development of the instructional program and acts as a guide for an evaluating team. At any time the local staff may wish to reshape the statement of the purposes of music in the school so that it is more compatible with current thought, student need, and social context. The philosophic statement should also reflect a portion of the overall educational position defined by the school system. The point of evaluation for the music education philosophy is the degree to which the program complements and realizes goals and objectives appropriate to the philosophical statement.

---

16 Charles Leonhard and Robert House, *Foundations and Principles of Music Education* (New York: McGraw-Hill Book Company, 1959), p. 357.

TERMINAL GOALS

Much has been written in this book regarding terminal goals. These are statements that describe in a *general* way the dimensions of music behavior of students upon graduation. Evaluators should be able to appraise goals in relation to a stated philosophic position defining the role of music in the school system. Terminal goals are the beginnings of operational statements of philosophy. On the other hand, both outside and local evaluation teams should have the opportunity to appraise students in relation to stated terminal goals. Because of the unique, nonverbal nature of some desired outcomes in music, provision should be made for a form of direct observational evaluation involving nonreactive measures.

COURSE DIVISION AND OBJECTIVES

In order to implement instructional programs that bring about the stated terminal goal, faculty decisions on the grouping of experiences are necessary. Performance experiences and nonperformance experiences provide one basic division. Decisions must be made about how many and what kinds of instrumental or choral ensembles are needed. The kind and frequency of humanities, general music, allied arts, and musicianship courses should be defined. The extent and presence of special features for the elementary program must be identified.

Basic objectives of performance classes usually reflect concern with music skill development, and rightly so. Nonperformance classes often include experiences that can be classified as performance but do not focus on skill development as an objective but rather as a means toward a more affective outcome. In any event, curriculum evaluators should be able to ascertain the contribution of each class or level to the overall goals of the music program.

CONTENT, SEQUENCE, AND INSTRUCTIONAL OBJECTIVES

Given program objectives for each course, individual faculty members make decisions on content, sequence, and appropriate daily, weekly, or unit objectives. Evaluators will want to assess the appropriateness of content and sequence in relation to specified program objectives. The proposed instructional sequence should progress smoothly and cyclically. Are all necessary learnings identified that will produce the level of competence thought desirable? Are these superfluous elements of sequence that will cause inefficiency in learning or teaching? Are means and ends clearly differentiated but rationally related? Are instructional objectives reasonable, precisely stated, and therefore assessable?

LEARNING EXPERIENCES

Persons charged with determining program effectiveness should visit actual classes or review instructional action plans. The plan should contain the nature of the learning experience. Evaluation from objective sources will aid in determining the effectiveness of any experience. Evaluators may wish to assess a given experience in relation to individual learning problems. Since learners achieve in different ways, a great variety of instructional format is possible. For example, listening perceptiveness developed through individualized instruction promises innovations in tailoring instruction to individual need. Experiences capable of being adapted to programmed learning formats should be identified and may become the subject of materials development.

The experiences the pupils have when confronting music are the very center of the music curriculum. It is only here that actual learning can take place. What the students do during a confrontation with music is the most important concern of a curriculum evaluator. The evaluator will simply have to go to classes to see what students do. He will look for variety, interesting repetition, and restrained teacher-centered activity. The focus will be on student activity, performing, creating, and listening.

SCHEDULING AND FACILITIES

Either a curriculum evaluation team or a local staff committee should exercise close scrutiny over scheduling patterns. Two schedule questions need answers: First, is the allotted time adequate to program? Second, are there reasons unique to music instruction that provide a rationale for special scheduling considerations? In addition, evaluators might wish to ask about grouping and its practice and effect on music learning.

Facilities for instruction should also be carefully appraised. What kind of sound reproduction equipment is available? What instruments are school-owned? What instruments are missing? Is the budget adequate for repairs, replacement, and capital outlay? What individual listening equipment is available to students? What kinds of instructional materials are available? Are quantities adequate?

PLANS FOR EVALUATION

Instructional staffs should be developers of student progress measuring instruments. These tests are constructed to measure program and instructional objectives. Given accurate measuring devices, evaluation of the instructional program is possible. The objective, disassociated viewpoint of evaluation teams can aid in decisions on the accuracy of measurement. Do the tests measure what they are supposed to measure (validity)? The effect of an instructional program on student behavior is the most important factor in assessing the impact and worth of the curriculum in music. Precise student evaluation has much to contribute to overall program evaluation. One author notes:

> Teacher-constructed tests are a necessity for evaluation in the cognitive area. Even if new standardized tests become available for this important area, these cannot completely replace teacher-constructed tests directed at the specific program of the local situation.[17]

The reasons for this position are obvious. Recalling Oliver's statement that teachers must be psychologically committed focuses attention on true investment in total instructional pattern. Developing measuring devices for all kinds of music instruction (affective, psychomotor, cognitive/perceptive) is a teacher or staff responsibility when published standardized measures will not suffice.

Similarly, overall program evaluation is an appropriate task for local music staffs. An often-used approach is the development of a rating scale of descriptive statements that could be rated on a 1–5 basis as follows:

Circle

disagree   agree

1 2 3 4 5   Program objectives for choral performance classes are clearly understandable.

1 2 3 4 5   Program objectives for choral performance classes are reasonable and attainable.

1 2 3 4 5   Program objectives for choral performance classes are appropriate to student need and ability.

---

[17] Richard J. Colwell, *The Evaluation of Music Teaching and Learning* (Englewood Cliffs, N.J.: Prentice-Hall, Inc., 1970), p. 81.

In any event, local music staffs may wish to construct a checklist or rating scale for their own use. One researcher developed a similar scale for evaluating music in the elementary school. Raters were asked to use the following continuum on several aspects of the school music program (example statements follow).

XX = if the provision or condition is made extensively.
X = if the provision or condition is made to some extent.
O = if the provision or condition is very limited.
M = if the provision or condition is missing and needed.
N = if the provision or condition is not desirable or does not apply.

(   ) A rote song repertoire includes enjoyable material which meets the growing needs, interests, and abilities of pupils.

(   ) Many and varied singing activities are provided which include folk and art songs.

(   ) At the advanced elementary levels pupils participate in a variety of part-singing activities.

(   ) Opportunities are provided for all pupils to participate in well-planned singing activities for assemblies and special programs.

(   ) A glee club or choir provides for pupils with special talent or interest.

(   ) How extensive is the *variety* of music activities to meet the music needs of all pupils?

(   ) How adequate is the *content* of music activities to meet the music needs of all pupils?

(   ) Instructional activities are planned in accordance with clearly defined objectives for music education.

(   ) Instructional activities interrelate all music activities (singing, playing, listening, rhythmic, and creative).

(   ) Instructional activities are based on recognition of individual differences.

(   ) A rote-song repertoire is presented as continuous or sequential music experience common to all levels of the elementary school.

(   ) How effectively do the methods of instruction meet the *group* needs of pupils?

(   ) How effectively do the methods of instruction meet the *particular* music needs of individual pupils?

(   ) To what extent do evaluation procedures help the pupil to understand the nature of his growth in music education?

(   ) Sets of school song books or worthy and enjoyable material are available.

(　) Supplementary song books are available on all levels.

(　) Teachers' manuals and accompaniment books for all sets of song books are available.

(　) A library of selected rote-song books is available.

(　) Books containing material on music history, composers, instruments, and stories are available.

(　) To what extent are pupils developing desirable instrumental knowledge and skills?

(　) To what extent are pupils developing self-expression through music?

(　) To what extent are pupils developing desirable knowledge and skills in music theory?

(　) To what extent are pupils applying their knowledge and skills in out-of-school music activities?

(　) To what extent are music activities making effective contributions to the total school program?[18]

Another facet of evaluation that belongs in an overall assessment plan for a music staff is a longitudinal study. A study of students from the beginning to the end of the instructional program is of great assistance in program development. Similarly, case studies of graduates who remain in the community could influence the redesign of the instructional program.

DEVELOPING CRITERIA FOR PROGRAM EVALUATION

As noted, program assessment can be effected by either inside or outside teams of evaluators. In many ways the process resembles a descriptive research problem of determining the status of the instructional program. This is precisely what curriculum evaluation attempts to do. A number of techniques are appropriate in securing data to support a status study. Not all will depend on the analysis of student behaviors through testing or observation. Tests can disclose evidence of unattained objectives but not the reasons why. Checklists, rating scales, observation report forms, and structured and unstructured interviews provide other materials helpful to program evaluation. A number of unobtrusive or nonreactive data-gathering techniques can also be used. Finally, curriculum outlines and statements of goals and objectives must be carefully

---

[18] Charlotte Fellman.

scrutinized. The following list of objective criteria may be valuable in the program evaluation process. The statements are an edited version of the material presented above (pp. 136–138).

Not   Clearly
Evident ⟷ Evident
1 2 3 4 5

Not   Clearly
Evident ⟷ Evident
1 2 3 4 5

Not   Clearly
Evident ⟷ Evident
1 2 3 4 5

I. Program

    A. The instructional program reflects logical commitment to stated goals.

    B. The instructional program includes balance among the several avenues of musical instruction.

    C. The instructional program is sympathetic to community need.

    D. The instructional program is continuous and articulated between instructional levels.

    E. The instructional program contains a plan for evaluation and regeneration.

    F. The instructional program is dynamic and can assimilate change.

II. Outcomes

    A. Goals and objectives are clearly stated.

    B. Program or course goals are appropriate to stated terminal goals.

    C. Goals and objectives are democratically derived with staff consensus.

    D. Goals and objectives describe capabilities exhibited by graduates.

    E. Goals and objectives reflect awareness and concern for student needs.

III. Learning

    A. Learning experiences relate to clearly stated instructional objectives.

    B. Learning experiences have a rational sequential organization.

    C. Learning experiences provide true opportunities for learners to confront music.

D. Learning experiences provide for all kinds of music learning.

E. Learning experiences allow for differences among students:
   1. culturally different,
   2. gifted performer,
   3. nonperformer,
   4. handicapped.

F. Learning experiences incorporate materials adequate for purposes of instruction.

IV. Environment and Staff

A. Instructional settings are adequate for instructional needs.

B. Financial support for the program is evident.

C. Instructional media and equipment are appropriate to needs.

D. Class scheduling facilitates instruction as well as possible reflecting administrative support.

E. The teaching staff is adequate to attain desired outcomes.

F. The teaching staff exhibits a spirit of cooperation evidenced by common concern for the instructional program and outcomes.

G. The teaching staff is afforded released time for evaluation, development, and implementation of the curriculum.

Many similar sets of criteria are available and can be adopted to local instructional programs. Leonhard and House have suggested an exhaustive list of guides for program evaluation. Included are:[19]

1. The controlling idea underlying the entire program is the development of musicianship and musical responsiveness.

2. The program operates on the basis of a well-formulated statement of objectives which are consistent with and contribute to the objectives of the school and which have been developed cooperatively by the music education staff.

3. The program is organized and operated to contribute to the stated objectives.

---

[19] Leonhard and House, *op. cit.,* p. 359.

4. The program exhibits continuity from the elementary school through secondary school.

Twenty-five statements are included. As Leonhard suggests, the statements represent *his* philosophical outlook on music education. These criteria are only included as a guide. There is no implication of primacy or idealness. Local staffs can readily develop a similar list of statements if a set of terminal goals is at hand. The principal purpose of program evaluation is to gather evidence that can assist in making decisions on the substance of the school music curriculum. Evaluation of student and program does in fact offer the best single means of fruitful program modification and a more efficient, ideal curriculum.

SUMMARY

The process of evaluation was identified as an integral part of the curriculum building process. The evaluation phase is in reality a descriptive research problem whereby data are collected to assess the efficiency and power of the instructional program to reach intended outcomes. Both student and program need careful appraisal. Student achievement could be based primarily on teacher-made criterion-oriented measures in relation to stated objectives. The instructional program can be assessed by curriculum experts by means of a checklist or similar evaluative tool. The product of a complete program of evaluation is information that provides for the modification, retention, or selected discontinuance of all or part of the instructional program.

ACTIVITIES FOR STUDY AND DISCUSSION

1. Gather data and develop a checklist of musical criteria which can be helpful in determining when a school music program needs reform.
2. Experiment in the development of an instrument to measure music preference.
3. Discuss the advantages and disadvantages of standardized vs. teacher-made tests.
4. Develop a checklist to evaluate an instructional program in music listening.
5. As a class project, visit a small community and assess the impact of the school music program on the community as a whole.

SUPPLEMENTARY READINGS

Colwell, Richard, *Evaluation in Music*. Englewood Cliffs, N.J.: Prentice-Hall, Inc., 1970.

Grobman, Hulda, *Evaluation Activities of Curriculum Projects: A Starting Point*. Chicago: Rand McNally & Co., 1968.

Lehman, Paul, *Tests and Measurements in Music*. Englewood Cliffs, N.J.: Prentice-Hall, Inc., 1968.

Tyler, Ralph W., Robert M. Gagné, and Michael Scriven, *Perspectives of Curriculum Evaluation*. Chicago: Rand McNally & Co., 1967.

Wilhelms, Fred T., ed., *Evaluation as Feedback and Guide*. Washington, D.C.: Association for Supervision and Curriculum Development, National Education Association, 1967.

index

Achievement tests, 118–19
Aesthetic education, 28
Affective domain, 70, 72, 73
Aims of education, 24, 25
Aliferis, James, 119
Aliferis Music Achievement Test, 119
Arberg, Harold, 15
Aural skills, 62

Balanced music program, 64
Banathy, Bela, 21, 27, 55, 117
Behavioral objective, 50–58
Behaviorism, 20, 21
Birge, Edward Bailey, 4
Bloom, Benjamin, 70
Broudy, Harry, 29
Bruner, Jerome, 102

Classroom experience, 81, 82
Colwell, Richard, 14, 76, 119, 134

Community:
  role in curriculum development, 30,
    31
Concept learning, 94–96
Concepts:
  defined, 94
  musical, 95
Content of instruction, 61–79
  classifying content, 69–76
  criteria for content, 62
  identifying content, 63–67
  objectives key to content, 68–69
Course of study, 15
Creativity, 82
Criteria
  for change, 17–18
  for objectives, 55, 59
Criterion-referenced test, 120
Curriculum:
  criteria for evaluation, 141–44
  evaluation of, 136–39
  music education, definition of, 1

Curriculum development (*see also* Program building):
  evaluation in, 37, 38
  general, 22, 23
  identifying content, 34
  process, 25–39
  role of research, 30–32
  teacher role, 39, 40
Curriculum guides, 15

Decision-making:
  content, 63, 78
  learning experiences, 62, 112
Descriptive research, 31
Discipline, 13
Doll, Ronald, 24

Earhart, Will, 6
Enjoying music, 13
Ernst, Karl, 11, 68, 69
Evaluation:
  affective domain, 123
  curriculum, 134–44
  knowledge, 122
  objectives as basis of, 117, 118
  reports, 129
  skills, 49, 122
  student, 116–34
  types of, 116
Experience:
  learning, 81, 82
  matrix for, 113
  selection of, 112
Experimental research, 32

Facilities, 138
Feedback:
  in learning, 86–94
Five-Year Study of the Musical Aptitude Profile, 14

Gagné, Robert, 85–90, 93, 94, 97–99, 101, 103
Gary, Charles, 11
General music:
  curricular change, 21, 14
  experiences in, 111, 112

Goals:
  affective, 47
  cognitive, 47–48
  defined, 43
  music education, 3–11
  psychomotor, 48
Gordon, Edwin, 14, 119
Grobman, Hulda, 135
Guides, curriculum, 15

Herrick, Virgil, 21, 49
Hills, Charles, 123, 130–33
Historical foundations:
  curriculum development, 20–22
  music education, 2–11
House, Robert, 28, 38
Humanities, 109

Individual differences, 112
Instructional module, 36, 110
Instructional objective:
  defined, 45–46
  writing of, 45–59
Instructional planning, 108
Instrumental music:
  classes, 109
  curriculum, 130–33
  objectives, 54–55
Iowa Test of Musical Literacy, 119
Item difficulty (test), 121, 122

Judgmental process for content, 66

Knowledge, 70
Knuth, William A., 119
Krathwohl, David, 77
Kyme, George, 28

Learning, 81–114
  conceptual, 94–97
  experiences (classification), 112
  human, 86–102
  music, 84
  principle, 97–99
  sequence in, 102
  strategies, 111
  structures, 103–8

Learning experiences:
  defined, 81
  types, 82
Leonhard, Charles, 28, 136, 143–44
Listening, 62–82

McConathy, Osbourne, 6
Mager, Robert F., 21, 50, 51, 53, 54
Mason, Lowell, 3
Mason, Luther Whiting, 5
Measurement:
  criterion-referenced, 118
  non-reactive, 123
  norm-referenced, 118
  problems of in music, 117, 118
  purpose, 117
  types, 116, 117
Murphy, Howard, 69
Music:
  growth in, 14, 15
  learning, 84
  nature of experience, 62
  perception, 74
  reading, 103–5
Musical Report Card, 49, 129
Music education:
  American, history of, 3–12
  goals, 3, 5, 6, 10, 11, 43
  identifying goals for, 46–48
Music Educators National Conference,
  8, 9, 11

Norm-referenced tests, 118

Objectives:
  as content, 68–69
  curriculum evaluation and, 137
  function of, 48, 49
  learning experiences and, 111, 112
  pupil evaluation and, 116, 117, 120,
    122
  taxonomies of, 69–76
  writing, 50–59
Objectives (instructional):
  evaluating, 55, 59
  function, 49
  qualities of, 50–55
  samples, 56–58

Objectives (program):
  defined, 43
  examples of, 44–46
Oliver, Albert I., 31, 134, 135

Packages, learning, 108
Perception:
  classification of, 74
  role in music learning, 22, 62
Performance (music):
  aimless activity of, 12, 13
  objectives, 44, 49, 54, 126, 128
Philosophy:
  goals and, 32
  music program, 10
  role of, 28
Popham, W. J., 21
Program:
  evaluation of, 134–36
  objectives, 43
  organization of, 108
  sequence in, 102–8
Program building in music education,
  29–38 (*see also* Curriculum development)
Psychomotor domain:
  evaluation of, 122, 133
  objectives of, 72, 73

Reimer, Bennett, 21, 68
Reinforcement in learning, 86–94
Reliability (test), 121
Research in program building, 30–33

School:
  community and, 30–31
  curriculum pressures, 23
  sociological setting, 31, 32
Sequence:
  and learning, 82
  simple-complex, 102–8
Simpson, Elizabeth, 74
Staff, 17, 39
Supervisor, music, 30
Systems approach, 21

Taba, Hilda, 21, 27, 63, 83
Task analysis, 103

Taxonomy of Education Objectives:
  affective, 72, 73
  cognitive, 70, 71
  psychomotor, 72, 73–75
Teacher:
  method, 108
  role in program development, 39
Tests, 116–25
  achievement, 118–19
  content of, 122–23
  criterion-referenced, 120–22
  norm-referenced, 118–20
  standardized, 119, 120
  teacher-made, 120–22
Textbooks, 23
Theories of learning, 84
Tyler, Ralph, 21, 24, 26, 82, 83

United States Office of Education, 15,
  20, 74
Unobtrusive measurement, 123

Validity:
  content, 122
  test, 121
Value, musical, 62
Vocal music curriculum, 109

Watkins-Farnum Performance Scale,
  119
Woodruff, Asahel, 21, 76

Yelon, Stephen, 21